W9-CFQ-892

Vote Yes for Libraries

To Pat Sandidge, Sara Bunnett, Susan Elgin
and all the other people
who worked so hard
for Measure B

Vote Yes for Libraries

A Guide to Winning Ballot Measure Campaigns for Library Funding

by
ANNE M. TURNER

McFarland & Company, Inc., Publishers
Jefferson, North Carolina, and London

ALSO BY ANNE M. TURNER

It Comes with the Territory:
Handling Problem Situations in Libraries
(McFarland, 1993)

Getting Political:
An Action Guide for Librarians and Library Supporters
(Neal-Schuman, 1997)

Library of Congress Cataloguing-in-Publication Data

Turner, Anne M., 1941–
    Vote yes for libraries : a guide to winning ballot measure
campaigns for library funding / by Anne M. Turner.
       p.   cm.
    Includes bibliographical references and index.
    ISBN 0-7864-0855-3 (softcover : 55# alkaline paper) ∞
    1. Public libraries—Public relations—United States.
    2. Public libraries—Political aspects—United States.
    3. Public libraries—United States—Finance.   I. Title.
Z716.3.T875   2000
021.7—dc21   00-29187

British Library cataloguing data are available

Manufactured in the United States of America

McFarland & Company, Inc., Publishers
  Box 611, Jefferson, North Carolina 28640
    www.mcfarlandpub.com

Acknowledgments

Nobody writes a book without a lot of help from their colleagues and friends. As it turns out, mine are legion. They include many people in Santa Cruz, starting with Pat Sandidge, the managing director of the Friends of the Santa Cruz Public Libraries, Inc., and Gail Pellerin, elections manager for the County of Santa Cruz. Pat Busch, the assistant county administrative officer, was my partner through many library funding crises and fortunately knows much more than I do about public finance. Susan Elgin, the library's assistant director, and Sara Bunnett, our longtime board member, were both crucial to our 1996 election victory and the hard work that followed it.

Gene Bregman, Santa Cruz's polling consultant, has answered an infinite number of questions with great good humor. Katherine Lew was assigned to the Santa Cruz campaign by her then boss, consultant Larry Tramatola. I am glad to say we became friends and colleagues.

Some of the material in this book is based on questionnaires filed by library directors for *Library Journal*'s annual report on public library referenda. Richard Hall initiated this series more than 10 years ago. In 1999 I joined him as the author of the article on operating budget elections, while he stuck with his favorite topic: measures to provide funds for constructing library buildings.

The reporting librarians (and some others) whom I interviewed by telephone where Ronnie Budge of Medford, Oregon; Ann Cousineau of Solano County, California; Colleen Foster of the Stockton–San Joaquin County Library, California; Beth Wheeler Fox of the Westbank Community Library in Austin, Texas; Anne Marie Gold, former director of the Contra Costa County Library, California; Judy Klapproth of Humbolt County, California; James LaRue, Douglas Public Library District in Castle Rock, Colorado; Mary Koster LeBoeuf, Terrebonne Parish Library in Huoma, Louisiana; Mary Mahoney of the Chelmsford Public Library in Massachusetts; Susan Priest of Washington County, Pennsylvania; David Noel of the Toledo–Lucas County Library in Ohio; Bill Urbizu of the Miami–Dade County Library in Florida; Earleen Warner of the Willmar Public Library in Minnesota; and Daniel Zack of the Gail Borden Public Library in Elgin, Illinois.

Finally, I would like to thank my mother, Jessie M. Tweedy, who moved to Santa Cruz only a month before the election in 1996 but still managed to turn out a substantial number of her new neighbors to vote yes for Measure B, and Steve Turner, to whom I am married. He is a professional writer whose editorial hand and thoughtful comments improved every page of this book. He is also very good with yard signs and writes terrific letters to the editor. I am a member of Local 7 (Santa Cruz–Monterey) of the National Writers Union and am grateful for the support the union gives every writer.

Anne M. Turner
Santa Cruz
February 2000

Contents

Preface
This Book Is
About Winning

Fresno (California) County librarian John Kallenberg tells the story of the campaign for a tax increase mounted by Fresno library supporters in 1986. They ran a shoestring effort because they were sure that people would resent and vote against any campaign for the library that smacked of political style, or seemed slick, or looked like anybody was spending money on it.

My library in Santa Cruz did exactly the same thing eight years later. Both Fresno and Santa Cruz lost— Fresno by only two points but Santa Cruz by a whopping 17 percent.

Santa Cruz returned to the voters in 1996 and Fresno in 1998, this time with carefully structured campaigns that targeted Yes voters based on professional polling and with strategy and tactics developed with the help of campaign consultants. Both won, getting more than the 66.6 percent of the vote required by the California super-majority law. Fresno's win is even more impressive than Santa Cruz's because Fresno County is very large, mostly rural, and economically more hard-pressed.

Vote Yes for Libraries is written for the library directors, staff, board members, and Friends who want to know how to go about winning a ballot measure election. It rejects the shoestring/grassroots approach to campaigning because that strategy is increasingly less likely to work.

Even in the best of economic times, persuading people to vote new taxes for library operating funds or buildings is a difficult business best aided by professional help. Library supporters, just like their counterparts raising money for the schools or any other public service, must learn better how to make the political process work for them and for their causes.

1

Sometimes public libraries are forced to go to the voters because of peculiarities of state law. In New York, for example, if a library (or other public agency) wants a budget increase, it must secure voter approval—even if the increase is merely to pay for a normal rise in the cost of living.

This puts tremendous pressure on the libraries in smaller towns and school districts to live within their existing budgets for two or three years in a row before returning to the voters for another increase.

In Texas there is no state or local legal mandate to fund public libraries at all. It was only recently that a mechanism (library districts) was established by the legislature so libraries could appeal to the voters for public support.

Other libraries must return to the voters for operating levy approval because they have won the popular vote once but not by enough to meet their state's "super-majority" rules. California, for example, requires a two-thirds majority to pass most tax measures, a stricture that has forced popular libraries, Contra Costa County Library for instance, back to the voters twice in two years. In Oregon a ballot tax measure may be passed by a simple majority, but the turnout on election day must be 50 percent plus one of all registered voters.

Across the country public libraries find themselves facing increased demands for services that are ever more expensive to provide. Gone are the days when their advocates could sit back and wait for the local funding authority to understand the need for more money or for the state legislature to allocate big chunks of revenue for new library buildings. Public library boards, supporting Friends organizations, and even staffs have found that they must become active players in the political process of local decision making. And matching budgetary need against political reality, advocates for library measures must go after a win using every tool available.

Election campaigns are complicated and messy and, despite their dependence on the calendar, distinctly nonlinear in nature. For example, a campaign organization should be well into raising money by the February before a November election. But you can't raise serious money without a well-defined campaign plan, and most organizations don't have a plan until they've hired a campaign consultant. They can't hire a consultant until they have raised enough money to be able to guarantee the consultant's fee.

The same goes for opinion polling, which is pretty crucial to both the plan and the decision to go to the voters in the first place. It is not a catch–22, but it surely can be confusing.

Constructing an orderly book that describes all the campaign elements and gives advice about making them work can be equally messy, but I have tried to organize things as logically as possible.

The first six chapters of *Vote Yes for Libraries* are devoted to precampaign activities: talking the local legislative body into putting the library measure on the ballot, forming a campaign committee, writing ballot language and arguments, conducting opinion polls, hiring a campaign consultant, and developing a campaign plan, budget, and calendar. There is a chapter on volunteers and then two more on that all-important subject, raising money.

The final five chapters are about the campaign itself: tactics such as Web sites and phone banks, handling the media and the opposition (which are not necessarily the same), and a final chapter on what to do if you lose.

My library has both lost an election and won one. I can say with great authority that winning is better, although there is a good deal to be said for what you can learn from a losing effort.

Although I have talked with library directors all over the United States, many of the examples in this book are from the Santa Cruz experi-

ence because it is the one I know the best. Also, the 1996 Santa Cruz campaign was a good example of what a bunch of largely inexperienced library supporters could accomplish once they decided to win.

So we've reached the standard point for hortatory apothegm: Anything worth doing is worth doing well. Winning isn't everything, it's the only thing (thanks, Vince Lombardi). Nothing ventured, nothing gained! Rock on! Buckle down, Winsockie, you can win! Act against the slings and arrows of outrageous fortune!

Learning political methods and taking political action actually can be fun. I found it so—exhausting, but fun nonetheless. Besides, you had nothing better to do with the next 10 months of your life, did you?

And may the Force be with you.

Twenty Useful
Campaign Terms

"A" LIST: The number-one or best list of contributors to political campaigns available in your area.

ASTROTURF: "The term describing those nice-sounding 'grassroots' organizations that are really just glorified P.R. fronts." *California Journal*, vol. 30, no. 6 (June 1999), p. 6. For example, the Pure Water Alliance could actually be a coalition of organizations opposing stringent antipollution regulations.

BASE VOTERS: Those voters who, based on performance in previous elections, are predicted to be highly likely to vote in favor of your measure.

BOND: A certificate of debt due to be paid by a government or corporation to an individual holder and usually bearing a fixed rate of interest.

CANVASSING: Going through a neighborhood soliciting votes. But also, polling or otherwise finding out the opinion of a specified group of people, e.g., canvassing the Illinois delegation at a political convention.

DAYS (OR WEEKS) OUT: The number of days (or weeks) left before the election, e.g., "We've scheduled the mailing to land twenty-two days out from November 3."

EARNED MEDIA: Press or media coverage for which the campaign doesn't pay. Evening television news coverage of the roof leak that has forced the closing of the Live Oak Branch, and interviews with anxious library users wondering when the library will reopen, is an example of earned media.

EMILY: Early Money Is Like Yeast.

ELAW: Everybody Loves a Winner.

GOTV: Get Out the Vote.

GRASS ROOTS: The people. A grassroots campaign relies heavily on volunteers rather than money.

LAND DATE: The date a piece of campaign literature arrives in the mailbox of a voter.

LITERATURE DROP: A mailing or a door-to-door distribution of campaign materials, usually used in a collective sense, e.g., "The campaign did three literature drops on the West Side."

MILL: "One tenth of a cent; used as a money of account, esp. in certain tax rates." (*Random House Dictionary* 1980).

MILLAGE: The tax rate, as for property, assessed in mills (i.e., tenths of a cent) per dollar.

TOP-LINE RESULTS: The first results from an opinion poll, reporting how many people responded negatively or positively to each question with percents of the total sample.

SWING VOTERS: Those voters who, based on performance in previous elections, may be persuaded to vote in favor of your measure.

TARGETING: "Targeting is the discipline that, through the study of past election results, polling data, demographics, and related information, helps a campaign determine which voters are worthy of attention and which are best ignored" (Catherine Webb and Josephy Mockus, "Recruiting and Managing Volunteers," Campaigns and Elections, *The Road to Victory 2000*, p. 610).

TRACKING POLLS: Opinion polls conducted during the campaign to measure changes in voter support.

WIFM: What's in It for Me

1
In the Beginning

Let's start with an assumption. Your library wants to go to the voters because you need tax money for operating funds or to construct a new building. In fact, the need is pressing, or else you wouldn't bother.

The need is *so* pressing that the library's leadership—the director, the members of the board, the Friends—are willing to invest major portions of their time and energy over the next many months trying to get the electorate to vote for the measure. You've walked and talked the library's need all over the community, and you believe you've built a consensus that something must be done.

Let's also assume that the library has a plan for the services it would like to be giving and a list of the physical assets needed: the ideal number of open hours, how big the materials budget should be, the components of the automation system upgrade, or the size of the new building.

The problem isn't the plan. Rather, it's that not everyone agrees that going to the voters is the right thing to do. And the most important group of the unconvinced comprises the elected officials (the city council, the county commissioners or the board of supervisors) who have the power to put the measure on the ballot.

It is not that they don't support libraries or even that they don't understand the library's needs. After all, they have been the recipients of the library's pleas, year after year after year, for enough money to provide the kind of services the people want.

The problem with elected officials is that they hear the same thing from every department, whether it is public works or parks and recreation. And for most of them libraries are nice enough institutions but not up there with fire or police in the ranking of crucial public services.

Elected officials also are acutely conscious of the public's real dislike of any proposal to increase taxes. That's why they almost invariably choose to twist the existing budget to fund streets and uniformed departments, leaving the library and the other "soft services" to get along as best they can. And because the first job of most elected officials is to get reelected, it is the rare county commissioner or city council member who is willing to propose going to the voters for a general tax increase that will solve all the jurisdiction's revenue problems.

This puts the library's advocates in the position of needing to persuade the council or the board of supervisors of at least three things: that a quarter-cent sales tax (or whatever) designated for the library will solve the library's

funding problems for a specified length of time, that this is the year to put the measure on the ballot, and that given the chance, the voters will vote for it. Library supporters also need to demonstrate they have the resources to mount an effective campaign.

Those are the topics of this chapter and the next one, with some added information about the final step the elected officials and the campaign advocates take to make it official: adopting ballot-measure language, writing the argument in favor of the measure and a rebuttal to the opposition's argument against.

This Is the Right Tax

Persuading the elected officials and everyone else that a tax measure on the ballot makes sense means explaining to them how much money is needed, deciding on the taxing mechanism, and agreeing on the duration of the tax.

HOW MUCH IS NEEDED?

Predicting how much a new building will cost is a fairly simple matter. By the time you are ready to discuss going to the voters, you certainly know whether this is a $15 million project that could be cut to $12 million, or a bottom line $10 million, take it or leave it (it's not worth doing if we don't build the whole thing).

Your jurisdiction's finance department people are the ones who

know the town or county's financial rating and therefore how much it is going to cost to borrow whatever millions for what length of time. They will figure out the amount the property tax is likely to increase per annum years ahead and therefore how quickly the bond is paid off. This information will probably come as amount per $1,000 of valuation and can later be translated into a campaign slogan such as "Pennies on the tax rate will buy books for our kids!" Later, if you win, the finance folks will even hire bond counsel to help borrow the money.

Setting the amount of an operating budget levy is a bit more complicated. Let's assume that you don't live in New York State or some other place where you must go to the voters every time you wish to increase the library's budget. Rather, your library's need is for long-term budget support—a new source of funding that will allow the library to restore or add services and meet the challenges of changing, growing public needs.

So you project a picture of ideal (or at least desirable) library services over the next five to seven years in terms that the elected officials will like. It's just another form of long-range planning but with price tags for the wish list.

Restoring or adding open hours would cost $65,000 in year one. Of course the book budget should be increased; probably existing staff could handle another $25,000 worth of items, but anything more than that will require more people in the cataloging department.

Upgrading the automation system is a top priority, probably costing $500,000. The library could borrow for it, spreading the cost over several years.

You have a list of deferred maintenance projects approximately a yard long—everything from rewiring so that the lights don't dim every time the fan in the staff bathroom is turned on to replacing the roof. You could easily spend $50,000 to $90,000 a year on these projects alone.

And the community desperately needs more services for teenagers, so the children's staff wants to establish an electronic homework center. That'll be another $30,000, which you think you can incorporate into the automation system upgrade.

Where the new staff is supposed to come from is another question.

Quite a few people would like to see the library open on Sunday afternoons, and you know you need somebody else on reference, plus, really the library ought to…

Well, you get the picture. Just make sure your figures are solid and the picture is ready to sell.

Next, make a chart that looks like Table A (next page), and start playing with some ballpark scenarios, such as increases ranging from 20 percent to 50 percent. Establish a revenue line across the top: existing funding in the first column plus new funding at a 20 percent increase. Inflate it across the table at 4 percent growth per year, which could be conservative or optimistic depending on where you live.

Put the existing budget in the Base Budget Line, and then begin plugging in numbers (in the Year 1 column) for the needed new services. Everything except Deferred Maintenance and Debt Service to pay for the automation system upgrade (which are fixed costs) becomes part of the Base Budget in the year after it is added.

The Base Budget inflates by 4 percent each year. And don't forget to inflate the cost of any new service for the years before you add it: what costs $25,000 in year 1 may well cost $27,040 by the time you get around to it in year 3. But inflation isn't increasing at 4 percent per year, you're thinking. Right, but experience says that there are likely many things you haven't thought of that are going to cost more money, so it is better to estimate on the high side rather than the low.

It doesn't take a math whiz to see

Table A

	Year 1	Year 2 +4%	Year 3 +4%	Year 4 + 4%	Year 5 + 4%
Revenue (existing plus new source @ 20% increase)	1,000,000	1,040,000	1,081,600	1,124,864	1,169,859
Base Budget	800,000	926,000	963,000	1,001,520	1,088,381
Restore—Open Hours	65,000	N/A	N/A	N/A	N/A
Increase Book Bud	25,000	N/A	N/A	N/A	N/A
Add Reference Staff	—	—	—	45,000	N/A
Deferred Maintenance	50,000	50,000	50,000	50,000	50,000
Debt Service	107,500	107,500	107,500	107,500	107,500
Total Budget	1,047,500	1,083,500	1,120,500	1,204,020	1,245,881
Revenue Less Budget	(47,500)	(43,000)	(38,900)	(79,156)	(76,022)

that a 20 percent increase in the budget isn't going to be enough to do what needs doing. In fact, it is grossly inadequate. You've already scrimped by putting the electronic homework center equipment into the automation system upgrade, which may well be smoke and mirrors. And waiting until year 4 to add more staff is also unrealistic.

With added open hours, new access to the Internet, and teenagers all over the place after school, it is obvious that you'll need more people sooner rather than later. So let's look at Table B, which shows a projection with a 35 percent increase.

The important point about these calculations is that they give you a realistic picture of what you can actually do. In the abstract a 35 percent increase in the budget seems like a tremendous amount—until you run out the numbers at 25 percent and 30 percent and realize that those increases just aren't enough. There are two other things to remember

about making these kinds of projections.

The first is to be honest and not embarrassed. If it is going to cost $65,000 to add staff for the additional open hours, say so. Don't cut it down to $50,000 and believe you'll be able to make it work somehow. And don't start apologizing for the cost of trained library staff. The fire chief isn't ashamed of the price of firefighters. Since the library workers are probably paid less, concentrate instead on explaining why you must have two people in the building whenever the library is open to the public.

The second thing to remember is that these plans and projections must be political. If you are going to go to the voters, and you want to win, you must include something for everyone, even if doing it isn't necessarily the most logical action in terms of library service.

Elected officials, who are the ones you are trying to persuade to put the measure on the ballot, can probably be

Table B

	Year 1	Year 2 + 4%	Year 3 + 4%	Year 4 + 4%	Year 5 + 4%
Revenue (existing plus new source @ 35% increase)	1,080,000	1,123,200	1,168,128	1,214,853	1,263,447
Base budget	800,000	925,600	973,024	1,043,145	1,099,431
Restore—open hours	65,000	N/A	N/A	N/A	N/A
Increase book budget	25,000	N/A	15,000	7,000	5,000
Add staff	—	10,000	15,000	—	6,000
Deferred maintenance	80,000	80,000	57,000	50,000	45,000
Debt service	107,500	107,500	107,500	107,500	107,500
Add Sunday hrs	—	—	—	7,000	N/A
Total budget	1,077,500	1,123,100	1,167,524	1,214,645	1,262,931
Revenue less budget	+2,500	+100	+ 604	+ 208	+ 516

made to understand the need to upgrade the automation system or fix the roof. But what they really see as first priority is more open hours at the branches in their districts and more books and magazines because they know that's what the public—their voters—want.

So if you want them to put your measure on the ballot, you have to give them those things. And you have to do it early in your five-year projection.

This is also a chicken-and-egg game. On the one hand, you have to figure out and say how much the library really needs. On the other, you know from opinion polling, or the stubborn (and loudly articulated) belief of several elected officials, that the people will never approve an amount that exceeds such and such per year. If that amount turns out to be only a 30 percent increase, go for it, but don't forget to be very clear about what the new money isn't going to buy.

WHAT KIND OF TAX?

Once you know how much money is necessary, you can look at the kind of tax that will raise it. You will certainly need help from the public finance mavens in the county treasurer's office or wherever. Someone with a computer and access to the tax rolls has to project, for instance, how much the property tax must increase if an additional $200,000 per year is to be raised for the library. In many places the property tax is the only option. In others sales taxes or special assessments are possible.

There isn't a taxing mechanism under the sun that doesn't come with its own set of disadvantages, ranging from the regressive nature of the sales tax to the impact of higher property taxes on people with fixed incomes. If you have full options in picking a tax, choose the one you think will be easiest to win.

And don't allow the aforesaid public finance mavens to make the decision for you. Their opinions will be highly conventional and probably uninformed by any political savvy. Instead, get advice from your favorite elected official. The opinion polling you have already done should also give you some help in making this decision.

The discussions about what kind of tax to seek are best conducted in private, among other reasons because controversy about going to the voters gets the campaign off to a poor start and makes fund-raising even more difficult than it is under the best of circumstances. Would you give $1,000 or more to somebody who said to you: "Well, we're advocating a quarter-cent sales tax, but one of the commissioners feels strongly it should be a property tax, so we just don't know yet— except we're sure there will be *something* on the ballot"?

How Long?

Sometimes law sets the duration of a taxing measure. In some states government agencies have to return to the voters for reapproval or change every five years. But if your state or locality gives you full options, make the decision by considering the following:

• Is there any known opposition to your measure? If there isn't, great. If there is, think about whether going for a short-term tax (five years instead of ten or fifteen), will increase your chances of winning. Frankly, any time less than five years is hardly worth the effort.

• How stable is your taxing mechanism? Sales taxes are a wonderful resource so long as the economy is strong or at any rate not in recession. But when recession hits, a library heavily dependent on sales tax revenue may find itself pushed to make budget cuts. A shorter duration sales tax has the disadvantage of forcing you back to the voters sooner. The advantage, however, is that it provides an opportunity for rescue if your community hits economic hard times. Making this judgment requires looking carefully at the structure of the sales tax itself: does most of the tax revenue come from big-ticket items (such as automobiles) that people will defer purchasing in a recession? Or is a substantial chunk raised from things people won't want to get along without—clothing, soft supplies, movie tickets, services?

• Do some careful thinking (and consultation with regional planners) about the future of your community. For example, if you live in a place that is ripe for suburban-type development, be very careful not to trap yourself in a tax measure that doesn't expire until long after your service population has doubled. Many currently rural areas and small towns within striking distance of big cities find themselves in this situation these days. The burgeoning population has to live somewhere, and people seem willing to drive astonishing distances between home and work. If home is going to be where your little library is, make sure you have left yourself some flexibility for increasing revenue to meet new demand.

• What do you plan to do with the new money? Is five years long enough to get everything done, or do you anticipate a major restructuring (new branches, new staff, etc.) that realistically is going to take a minimum of 10 years to accomplish? You don't want to put the library in the situation of having to go back to the voters before you have had a chance to do what you promised you'd do in the tax election.

Obviously, duration of the tax measure is not a simple decision. Anyone's instinct is to want the darn thing

to last as long as possible so that you don't have to go through the campaign effort again.

In Santa Cruz in 1996 we got all kinds of sensible advice about how long our sales tax measure should last, including "Get it down below 10 because single digits are always preferable to voters." In the end we went for 16 years. Why 16? Three reasons. Sixteen years is the maximum allowed by California law. Sixteen years would place the renewal in a presidential (high-turnout) election year. And, probably most important, 16 years would be several years after the assistant county administrator and I (who ended up making the decision) planned to retire.

This Is the Right Year

It used to be conventional wisdom that tax measures, whether property or sales, are easier to pass when voter turnout is low. This wisdom rests on the logic that the advocates of the measure will work hard to get their supporters to vote and pray hard that the opposition will be too bored or lazy to do the same. In a high-turnout election, the theory goes, both sides will be voting. Also, the tax measure runs a strong chance of getting lost in the "big issues."

On the other hand, recent research suggests that low-turnout elections favor the positions of economic conservatives, who, as committed political participants, never fail to vote and vote no on issues such as the tax increases

Two Important Definitions

The date for holding a "regular election" is prescribed by law. For example, national congressional elections are held on the first Tuesday in November in even-numbered years. A higher number of voters tend to turn out for regular elections.

The date for holding a "special election" is *not* prescribed by law. Special elections are held at the direction of a local governing body such as the city council or a school board. Fewer voters tend to turn out for special elections.

that they despise. Progressives or moderates are the ones who are not turning out in low-turnout elections.

Fred Register, a political consultant in Southern California, points out that high- and low-turnout elections each have their advantages (and disadvantages).[1]

In a high-turnout regular election, there is lots of other stuff going on, so a tax measure runs much less risk of becoming the controversial issue that the electronic media falls on and plays up. The problem with running in a high-turnout election is that it is harder to raise money and get big-name supporters because everyone else—the candidates and the other issues on the ballot—is also trying to do the same thing and get the same people.

A low-turnout special election makes raising money and getting supporters easier but also makes the proposed tax measure highly vulnerable to attacks in the media from the opposition.

Register's comments came in the wake of a disastrous special election in San Diego in March 1999, when a county-wide sales tax measure for library services went down, getting only 50 percent of the vote (it needed 66.7 percent to pass). The San Diego measure was defeated by an antitax coalition that created a controversy in the last two weeks before the vote and used TV and radio news to exploit it (see chapter 13). But if the San Diego libraries had been on the ballot in the regular election the previous November, they'd have been up against a school bond measure and a highly contentious stadium question.

So the library supporters gambled that they could win a special election and ended up trapped in "there's nothing else going on" media coverage.

I am not sure that the media-market difficulties that plagued San Diego in 1999 are as big a factor for libraries serving regional hinterlands or small towns without multichannel TV outlets of their own. In those places high-turnout elections offer a distinct advantage because public libraries are such apple pie institutions. Virtually every other government agency has enemies with the exception of the fire department. Some people wouldn't pay a dime for more police. And although Americans support education, they have a terrible record supporting the school districts that provide it. But luckily for us, almost everybody loves libraries.

So it is generally to the library's advantage to be on the ballot, even with a tax measure, in a high-turnout election. It is to the library's advantage unless there is another highly controversial issue on the same ballot that is going to draw legions of anti-tax, antigovernment voters to the polls.

And finally, there is one other question about election timing that must be confronted: who pays? Occasionally a library's funding need is so great and so immediate that it has no choice but to request that a special election be called in its district. The trouble is that the beneficiary of the special election is usually required to pay for it. How much that costs depends on the size of the community:

$7,000? $15,000? Ask the county elections commission or the clerk.

If the library measure wins, the election cost can often be taken off the top of the new funds. But if it loses, and the library must pay out of its existing budget, it is deeper in the hole than ever. Sometimes the cost of a special election can be shared by two or more benefiting agencies, but then the library may be in the wretched business of asking voters to choose between equally worthy causes.

The Voters Will Vote for It

Opinion polling—the data gathering you *must* do in all but the smallest communities before you undertake a ballot measure campaign—is discussed in chapter 3. Solid numbers from a professional polling consultant are one of the strongest arguments you can present to persuade elected officials that the library measure is worth putting on the ballot. And if you have the numbers, but they aren't very solid, you probably shouldn't be attempting a ballot measure. The definition of *solid* is at least 60 percent in most places and 70 percent in California, where a "super-majority" of two-thirds is required to win.

Absent polling data, you can attempt to demonstrate the depth of library electoral support by mounting a letter-writing campaign (to both the newspapers and the elected officials). Another tactic is to turn out a crowd for a county commissioners' meeting several weeks *before* the library ballot measure proposal is on their agenda. Then during the "open microphone" portion of the meeting, library advocates get up and talk about the library's funding needs, plans for the future, and the average citizen's willingness to pay for good library services.

Democratic society or no, the truth is that by the time an elected body actually holds a public discussion on a yea-or-nay issue like placing something on the ballot, its members have usually made up their minds. So the library advocates need to make their point early in the process, before the officials' opinions are set. Advocates also need to be there on the day the measure is considered and put on another show that demonstrates how right the commissioners are to be agreeing to the proposal.

The elected officials, who have run for office themselves and know a good deal about just how much work is involved in winning, will also want to assess whether the advocates of the library measure are well enough organized, and sophisticated enough about campaigning, to win. That is the subject of the next chapter.

A Precampaign Nightmare

You're the library director. You've been working steadily and hard for the last six months putting together consensus that the sensible way to solve the library's long-range funding problem is to go to the voters with a designated tax measure. Opinion polling has established that the library can win, and a campaign committee is in place and has begun to raise money. Campaign consultants have been interviewed, and next week the county commissioners are set to make the final ballot placement decision.

You pick up the newspaper one morning, and there on page 3 is a story featuring the chair of the library board saying that he thinks it might be a good idea to form a coalition with the schools people and go to the voters for a shared tax measure. After all, libraries and schools are birds of a feather, aren't they?

The reporter has called up one of the county commissioners, who opines that it might be a good idea. Has the library looked into it, the commissioner wonders? Furthermore, local antitax honcho Sam Simple, whom the reporter also called (it must have been a really slow news day), has declared this the greatest inspiration since the Boston Tea Party: "If the public schools and the public libraries would just get together we taxpayers could save millions of dollars."

From the library's perspective there are approximately 6,000 things wrong with this idea, not the least of which is that sharing the proposed new tax would substantially cut into what the library needs and not do much for the schools either. But before you put together a damage-control strategy, you call the library board chair to find out where in the world he got this idea and why he is bringing it up now of all times.

The board chair is a little embarrassed but not cowed by the question. His version is that the reporter floated the idea of combining with the schools, and he was merely commenting. But it isn't really unthinkable, is it? "If we combined with the schools wouldn't we increase our chances of winning in November?"

No, you say, and explain that four months ago you and the superintendent of schools got together and explored this very scenario. You went over the dollar numbers of the proposed tax measure (which your polling results indicate is the maximum the voters will approve) and agreed that combining forces wasn't worth it to either the schools or the library.

"Besides," you say to the chair, "the schools bring a lot of baggage with them when they join you. Some people think they are really messing up. They are always begging for more money, but the kids don't seem to be getting a better education. I think they'd do us more harm as partners than good."

You and the chair agree that the coalition idea needs to be nipped before it has a chance to fully bloom. You decide to call the superintendent and see if you can persuade her to take the lead in quashing the whole thing. Hers is an elected office, and consequently she has better access to the local paper's managing editor.

The superintendent agrees, and soon enough the paper is running a front page interview (with picture) about how the schools love their partnership with the local public library but really need far more money than a share of the proposed tax measure will provide.

This is a nightmare because it demonstrates how very easy it is for the most carefully wrought political agreements to fall apart. Elected officials are like average voters writ large: a tad more sophisticated, perhaps, but as readily seduced by a seeming easy fix as anyone else. What a deal! Schools and libraries in the same cornucopia! Eventually, they would probably see the light but not before unneeded delays in getting the campaign off the ground.

There are also two lessons to be learned from the story. One is to spend some of that time you lie awake at night cataloging what you *haven't* told your board chair, and then make sure you fill in his or her information blanks. In this case having yourself disposed of the "coalition with the schools" idea early on, you never

thought anymore about it. But as a seeming easy fix, it has charm, including to the board chair who'd never heard it before. It is your fault he didn't have the facts when confronted by a reporter.

The second lesson is an old one: always look gift horses in the mouth. Before you form a coalition with anyone, take a very, very hard look at what they are bringing with them to the table. Even groups with whom you have natural alliances may be exactly the wrong folks to associate with in an election campaign.

A final comment: what about that newspaper reporter who went out fishing for a story? Did her editor send her? Before many more weeks pass, and the campaign gets into high gear, you and the board chair might well pay a visit to the managing editor to feel out the paper on its support and perhaps give the editor a background briefing on the ballot measure strategy.

Meeting with editorial boards is discussed in chapter 12. If the reporter normally covers the city or county political beat, ask that she be included. Your task is to lay some groundwork for the future and to make at least two things clear: that the campaign is open for business and planning to win, and that you library people are smarter than they think.

Getting Organized and Making It Official

If you go to a campaign training institute, or read any of the excellent books cited in the Note on Sources or endnotes, or listen to the advice you are given by every supporter from the mayor to local sportswriters, you know that the library campaign should *get organized*. You need a chair, a treasurer, and people for all the special campaign jobs, such as fund-raising and volunteer recruitment. Actually, however, finding these people isn't the issue.

What is really important is figuring out how to make the human resources you have in hand work into a campaign organization. The books and the training institutes give you very solid advice about setting up the campaign committee, finding just the right people for leadership and so forth. What they forget is that the group of people who put together the library measure proposal, and are trying to talk the elected body into placing it on

the ballot—usually the library board and the Friends organization—are already there.

As good-hearted and enthusiastic as these people may be, they rarely have campaign experience. Some may turn out to be very quick studies, but others won't be able to cope at all.

However, the county commissioners or the city council want to know whether the advocates for the library measure have the capacity to run an effective campaign. Do the library people have a committee in place? What is the campaign plan? Has the committee raised any money yet? Basically, their question is, "If we agree to put this measure on the ballot, are these folks competent to go out and win, or are we going to be embarrassed by a terrible defeat?"

It's a fair question. Although agreeing to put the measure on the ballot isn't the same as actually supporting it, in the public mind the connection is clearly there. The elected officials don't want to put themselves in the position of appearing to think something is a good idea, only to have it flame out at the ballot box.

So library advocates have to do their very best to appear competent, organized, and ready to go, whether they are or not. If the commissioners actually (and extraordinarily) agree early in the election-year cycle to place a measure on the ballot (say January for a November election), this may be difficult to do. The campaign committee is just getting organized, and no serious fund-raising has taken place.

One patch-over for this difficulty is to get your best-known and politically knowledgeable supporter (former Mayor Brown or retired State Senator Blunkett) to take the lead in front of the electeds. This person will give your nascent campaign the imprimatur of known expertise and success.

A much more usual scenario is for the elected body to delay placing the measure on the ballot until the last possible minute—usually for reasons related to the demands of their continuing agenda. This isn't necessarily a problem if their eventual action is a foregone conclusion. It gives the library leadership plenty of time to turn itself into an organized campaign: to form a campaign committee, begin raising money, hire a consultant, develop a campaign plan, and generally do all the advance work that conveys the impression of a confident and winning operation.

Notes on the Campaign Committee

Given that there is already a library leadership group in place, the persons who are doing the initial thinking for the library campaign—the board chair, the Friends president, even the library director—have the task of maneuvering the right people into taking on key jobs at the same time that a role is found for every current activist. This isn't easy, of course.

One way to make it work is to get the key group together and have a frank discussion (in private, of course) about the kind of campaign that is going to be mounted. What are people's expectations? Are we willing and able to contemplate a full-bore campaign?

Are we going to raise the money required to hire professionals where we need them and pay for high-quality materials? Honestly, now, do we plan to win or don't we think we can?

The answers to these questions will set the pattern for the whole campaign, which is why it is important—indeed *crucial*—that they be addressed at the start. Campaigns are hard work. They make tremendous demands on everyone's spirit, temper, and energy. If the campaign starts with disagreement about the basics and leaves such questions unresolved, it is doomed to failure. If it is a small town and the "vote" is six to one for a volunteer/grassroots effort, that may work. But in a larger jurisdiction that's the signal that some serious education is needed within the committee—or perhaps there shouldn't be a campaign this year.

Despite the advice from most experts that there be a single person in charge, most local-issue campaigns end up being run by a group of three or four people who meet frequently, make decisions collectively, and develop individual areas of special responsibility. Often the group is composed of one or two people from the library board and the Friends organization, the director, and a person who ends up being the campaign's volunteer coordinator and primary field organizer. The campaign chair is often a titular head, someone well known in the community who is recruited to lend his or her name and contribute money but who doesn't want to take day-to-day responsibility for any actual campaign work.

The campaign treasurer—the person who signs the checks and, just as important, signs the contribution and expenditure reports that the campaign must periodically file—is another person who doesn't *have* to be in the core group. He or she can be a local attorney willing to lend his or her name to the campaign and its letterhead, while one of the other key people does the actual bookkeeping work. But she or he must be confident of the integrity of the person doing that.

The library director plays a peculiar role in all this. On the one hand she or he knows more about library services and funding than anybody else on the committee and therefore is a crucial resource and well qualified for decision making. But the director is very likely prevented by law from working on the campaign during regular business hours—which makes for a lot of lunchtime and after-work campaign committee meetings. In a highly visible campaign the director's role often becomes a game: everyone knows, but no one admits, how important she or he is, and most people end up closing their eyes to the amount of time she or he is putting into the campaign.

In some respects the law makes perfect sense. Why should the taxpayers subsidize one side of the campaign—via the director's salary—and not the other? The reality, however, is that a library measure that does not have the full backing and participation of the director and other library staff is not going to win.

A warning is important here: if your campaign has a strong and well-organized opposition, be very careful about the staff's activities. The last thing the Yes campaign needs is to find itself in court defending the director against campaign violation charges, or worse, see its election victory declared invalid because of illegal campaign activities.

Making It Official

The last step the governing authority takes in putting a measure before the voters is to adopt the actual ballot language—what the voters will read in their absentee or sample ballots or at the polls on election day. Drafting this language can involve complex negotiations among several parties, including the county counsel or city attorney, the campaign consultant, and anyone else with strong opinions who wants to play. Then there is the drafting of the Argument in Favor of the measure and the construction of a rebuttal to the opposition's argument against.

WRITING BALLOT LANGUAGE

When you write the words that will actually appear on the ballot as the library measure, you strive mightily to ensure they make sense. What you want is for the average voter to spot your measure and say, "Oh yes, here's the library. I'll certainly vote for that." Alas, however, the brevity of the language allowed, and the number of people who want to participate in its drafting, can conspire to produce a product that *must* be known by its alphabetical designation (e.g., Measure B) because nothing else about it is understandable.

The county elections clerk, supported by the State Elections Code, makes most of the regulations that govern elections. Among these is the number of words a ballot measure may

have, as well as the counting rules. The latter can be critical. For example, is "County of Mesa Vista" one word or four? How many words are in "March 31, 2002"? Even with generous counting rules, saying what you want to do (levy a quarter-cent sales tax), how long it will last (10 years), who is going to do it (the board of county commissioners), and what the money will be used for (books, open hours, children's services) is not easy in only (for example) 75 words.

The drafting process is made even more difficult by the honest and correct desire of the responsible city attorney or county counsel to cover every conceivable legal base. The campaign consultant, on the other hand, wants something snappy, if ballot language can ever deserve that description: 75 words that make clear what an absolutely terrific idea Measure B is. The result can be dueling drafts such as the following, from the 1996 Santa Cruz County election:

From the county counsel:
Shall Ordinance No. 1 of the Santa Cruz County Public Library Authority be approved to provide needed funding to support and maintain local public libraries and library services through the acquisition of books, educational materials, technology, and computers, the improvement of educational and other library programs, and to repair, upgrade and expand library facilities by levying a ¼ of 1% local sales tax for a maximum period of 16 years to replace the existing ½ of 1% local sales tax when it expires on March 31, 1997.

And from the campaign consultant:
To provide needed funding to maintain local Public Libraries, to acquire books, educational materials, technology, and computers, to improve educational programs for children, adults and seniors and to repair, upgrade, and expand libraries shall the Santa Cruz County Public Library Authority adopt an ordinance levying a one-quarter percent County transactions and use sales tax to replace the existing one-half percent sale tax when it expires on March 31, 1997?

The consultant acknowledged that his language was perhaps a bit contorted, but as he pointed out, you always put what the money will do at the top. The board of supervisors adopted the county counsel's version, among other reasons because they didn't have the consultant's text in front of them.

Luckily, however, that formulation turned out to have too many words, so a compromise, incorporating the language from the consultant, was what finally appeared on the ballot. The supervisors adopted the replacement language in the last hour before they adjourned for a month-long summer vacation.

There are two rules to remember about ballot language. *First* is to start drafting (or push the appropriate legal authority to start drafting) at least two months before the governing board will take action. This way there is plenty of time to resolve the inevitable conflicts between needed legalese and readability. And don't be surprised if you have trouble getting the county counsel or whoever to take you seriously about the need for an early start. Theirs is an arcane world of torts and claims. They tend to forget that since

voters don't understand legal language, campaign professionals will have strong and legitimate ideas about how to present the measure.

Second, as already noted, begin with what the measure will do. It may well be true, as many campaign consultants say, that most people don't bother to read the actual ballot measure, even in the leisure of a prevoting perusal of the sample ballot they receive in the mail. But given that there must be a written statement of the measure, write the language for the 1 out of 50 voters who *will* read it. Make sure that the word *library* appears in the first line, not just the first sentence. Say what the money will do, and then say what kind of tax and how much.

WRITING BALLOT ARGUMENTS

When the county commissioners, board of supervisors, or whoever take the legal action to place a measure on the ballot, they start the election clock ticking. Everything from programming voting machines to the dates for filing campaign financial reports will now be scheduled in a time line set by the person in charge of elections.

State law may establish the election clerk's power, but it is driven by mundane realities, such as how long the county's contract printer needs to produce 100,000 twenty-page sample ballots. The schedule is achieved by counting backward. If election day is November 3, then the absentee ballots must be mailed on, say, September 23 so that they "land" (e.g., are delivered) no later than October 1. This means the printer must deliver them to the mail house by September 15, which in turn means the printer needs final proof not a day later than September 1, etc. And don't forget the federal Labor Day holiday in there somewhere.

The clerk is therefore likely to set extremely tight deadlines for the submission of ballot arguments in favor and against the measure, followed by another close deadline for rebuttals. In Santa Cruz in 1996 there were only 15 days between the meeting at which the supervisors placed the measure on the ballot and the date the argument in favor (350 words with five signatures) had to be filed. Then there were 12 days to file a rebuttal (250 words and five signatures) to the opposition's argument against the measure. The counting rules were the same as for the ballot measure itself.

Writing the text for the argument isn't particularly difficult. You set out what the measure is going to do to improve (or save) library services, without the legalese that complicated the ballot measure.

Try to anticipate and answer the points likely to be raised by the opposition, without actually stating the argument against. For example, "Local funds already going to libraries will *not* be reduced."

State exactly what the measure will do: "Expand services to children, including homework centers" or "Restore lost hours and extend weekend hours." Using a bulleted list is a good idea because it creates open space on an otherwise dense page of text.

Don't patronize the voter, but do try to use simple, clear language pitched at the level of daily newspapers. The campaign consultant will have a good deal to say about how the Argument in Favor should be written and what it should cover.

Campaign Consultant Catherine Lew says that not only do people rarely read the ballot language, but they also ignore the arguments. They *do*, however, look to see who signed the arguments in favor and the arguments against a measure. Therefore, people with impressive sounding titles should be asked to sign the argument.[1] Campaign Co-Chair Fred Smith may be a nice fellow, but probably only 200 people in the whole county have ever heard of him. Identifying him as a "Local Business Owner" makes him sound like the salt of the earth (which he is), but it won't cut much with most voters. Try for the president of a well-known organization such as the League of Women Voters, retired judges, or the former mayor of one of your service area towns.

It is probably wise to stay away from people whose titles indicate their political ties (e.g., Chair, Democratic Central Committee is not such a hot idea unless you can get the Republican chair as well). But don't hesitate to ask people with known party alliances (say the president of the Chamber of Commerce) to balance the ticket. You want to convey widespread support from known community leaders.

Gathering the signatures for the Argument in Favor is invariably a very laborious task. For one thing, the elections clerk will have an official form on which the signer must print and sign his or her name. For another, half the people you need for signatures will be away on vacation or otherwise inaccessible, especially if your measure is on the November ballot and you are thus doing this work around the Fourth of July weekend.

The other half will insist, quite reasonably, on seeing the text of the argument before they actually sign. But the argument text may not be ready until a day or two before it is due, which has campaign workers chasing down signatures at the last possible minute.

It is nice to think that the people collecting signatures for the Argument Against your measure are having just as hard a time as you are, but it probably isn't true. Your support is countywide, and therefore your supporters live all over the place. The opposition, however, may be a tightly knit group of naysayers who have coffee together every morning down at Mo's Diner. They simply passed the signature form around the table after they whipped up their 350 negative words.

WRITING THE REBUTTAL

Once the filing deadline is past, the elections clerk will release the Argument Against, and you can see who signed it and what the opposition is going to argue from now until election day. Just as your argument in favor sets out the bones of your campaign message, so will that of the opposition.

Now you know what you'd suspected—they are going to argue government waste. It is not that they are against libraries. Oh no, what they oppose is the taxes and regulations that create a supposedly hostile business climate. And if it is somewhat heartening to learn that the opposition didn't have anyone to tell them not to use words such as *disingenuous*, remember that as few people will read their Argument Against as read yours in favor.

The next step is to draft a Rebuttal, which probably has fewer words. The term *rebuttal* implies that you are answering the Argument Against, but in fact that is not necessarily the case. It may well be that the smarter thing to do is to ignore the opposition altogether and write a shorter positive pitch for your measure. Deciding on which strategy depends on what the opposition has said. If their argument is rife with misstatements of fact and outright lies that are easily refutable, go ahead and write a rebuttal that sets the record straight.

In San Diego in 1999 the opposition to the library sales tax measure made the mistake of using bad facts. Their Argument Against declared that there are no standards for public library services, and therefore the proponents could not argue that San Diego County libraries do not meet national standards of library service. The Yes on L campaign decided to sue, citing the American Library Association's *Minimum Standards for Public Library Systems, 1966*. They won, and the offending statement in the Argument Against was blacked out in the final ballot package.

If, however, the Argument Against is merely a series of assertions along the lines of how taxes are bad and the government wastes money, you might well ignore it. Start your Rebuttal with a sentence such as "Library opponents wrote their argument without checking their facts. The truth is…" and segue into a restatement of what your tax measure will creatively do with the funds—the basic campaign message.

One thing you can do with the Rebuttal is to get five new people with equally important-sounding titles to sign. This may mean (as it does in California) going back to your original signers and getting them to agree in writing *not* to sign the Rebuttal, thereby doubling your work. But changing the names has the effect of broadening the image of your measure's support, so it may well be worth the effort.

A Ballot Argument Nightmare

The phone rang at 9:30 A.M. on Saturday morning, just as Library Director Bill Shaffer was finishing a second cup of coffee and the morning paper and wondering if he could possibly get away with *not* mowing the back lawn today because the temperature would be in the high nineties, far too hot for serious exertion. The call was from Charlotte Mendoza, his board chair.

"It's happened," said Charlotte. "That idiot Marcia Laughton just called me. She wants her name taken off the ballot Argument."

"*What? Why?*"

"She says Grand River isn't mentioned specifically in the Argument, and anyway, it all looks 'too political.' She doesn't think the library should be involved in such a political effort, and she doesn't want to be associated with it."

"But that's crazy! She knows how taxes get passed. *She's* the former county commissioner and the most political person signing! And *none* of the towns are mentioned by name—it's a county-wide measure."

"I know, I know. But look, isn't it too late? I mean, yesterday at 5 P.M. was the filing deadline. Surely we can't change the Argument now."

"No, I don't think we can. And I certainly can't check it on a Saturday. This has to wait for Monday. Maybe she'll reconsider. Did she sound at all flexible?"

"Marcia? Old Ironsides? No, she didn't sound flexible. She sounded brassed off, as they say."

"#$%^! You know, this could be disaster. We're just getting started. We don't want to begin the campaign with a mess in the papers about how one of the Ballot Argument signers doesn't actually support the measure. And Marcia is just the kind of person who would buy a big display ad to make her point."

"You know," said Charlotte, "I really wonder what this is about. Maybe for all that farewell stuff she did about how she finally has time to spend with her grandchildren, she is missing being in office and having power. Maybe she just wants special attention and the library campaign is getting her anger because we happened to ask her for something at the right—or wrong—moment."

"So...?"

"So let's see. What could we do? Well, one thing is I could call up Tony Wachel and ask him to phone her. They used to be best friends and allies and he's still a commissioner."

"And he'd say what?"

"Oh, he'd thank her for signing the Ballot Argument. Say how crucial it is for important community leaders like her to march at the head of the parade on big issues even when they are out of office. That kind of stuff. It's worth a try, anyway. Besides, I can't think of anything else to do ... unless ... well, we could take the whole campaign committee over to her house on Sunday afternoon and do a little collective groveling."

"Naw. Try the Wachel approach first," sighed Bill. "We'll save groveling as a last resort."

The members of any campaign committee who have just spent three weeks running around the county collecting ballot argument signatures for a 5 P.M. Friday deadline are entitled to consider doing grievous bodily harm when one of the signers demands, *after* the deadline, to withdraw. Fortunately for the back-pedaling Laughton, this campaign is blessed with a board chair whose instinct is to think and analyze first. Mendoza's first guess about Laughton's motives may well be right, and if they are, deploying someone to thank her for her efforts might be just the right tactic.

If it doesn't work, and Laughton sticks with her demand that her name be stricken from the ballot Argument, the campaign should develop a unified line for public consumption on what happened and why. Something like, "Yes, it's too bad. We had a misunderstanding about how the measure applied to all library branches, not just hers. She says she'll vote for it, but she doesn't want to be a sponsor, so of course we agreed to remove her name." End of discussion.

The point of this nightmare is to remind us that in any campaign (not to mention much of life) what can go wrong most probably will. It is why some people find electoral politics so exciting. The worst and the best in people come out, and whichever happens to prevail at any given moment, the campaign committee has to deal with it.

3

Will They Support It?

So there you are at the reference desk or in line at the supermarket, and what everyone says to you is, "*Yes*, we love the library. Of course we'd vote for more money to support it. We wish you'd open on Sunday. You'd buy more best-sellers, wouldn't you?" And you get the same kind of response every time you talk to the Soroptimist Club or go to an event at your daughter's school.

The problem, of course, is that the people you are seeing on a daily basis are the choir: library users, the parents of library users, or the folks who volunteer or work in the library. All of these people have an investment in seeing the library provide more services. But they are not necessarily the majority of voters who have the final say on a new tax for the library. Before you can persuade your local elected officials to place a tax measure on the ballot, or indeed before you go to the trouble of mounting a petition campaign yourself, you *must* know whether the majority of voters will vote for it.

Furthermore, you need to know what kind of tax they favor (property? sales? special assessment?), the maximum amount the tax can be, how long it should last, and what particular library interests will persuade people to vote yes.

Getting this information is what polling is all about. Polls represent a window on public opinion. If the sample and the questionnaire are carefully constructed, or the focus group well managed, they are highly likely to present accurate information about what people think at the time the poll is conducted. While people's minds can be changed by the content of an election campaign or by any number of events, catastrophic or otherwise, collecting polling data is worth the effort because it gives guidance on the task that must be accomplished.

Two types of research methods are used extensively in election campaigns today. One, telephone polls, which collect *quantitative* data, are used before the campaign starts, and (if the campaign is rich enough) in the middle, and in the last days before the election. Focus groups gather *qualitative* information and are probably most useful in determining the content of campaign messages. This chapter will discuss both types of polling.

First, however, let us note another important reason for conducting an opinion poll, especially a quantitative one such as a telephone poll. Opinion polls are a tool that both elected officials and the news media understand and use. When a library presents polling data showing strong public support for its services, it is using a far more effective argument than the usual circulation or reference query data.

Why is a poll more effective? Because while in-house measures may be important benchmarks to you, they have no context in the minds of politicians and reporters. The response is likely to be "So what? 750,000 checkouts a year? Is that *it*, when you've got all those books?" But if you tell them that 75 percent of registered voters view cuts in library service as an important public issue, you are talking in a language an elected official understands.

Telephone Opinion Polls

It is estimated that most candidates for governor or senator, and often those for Congress or the state legislature, spend as much as 10 percent of their total campaign budget for opinion polling. And the pollsters themselves have become important members of candidates' consulting teams. In the library world we are not quite to that level of dependence on highly refined research data, but we do often require professional telephone opinion polling if we are to mount serious (that is, winning) election campaigns.

HOW MUCH DOES A POLL COST, AND WHO PAYS FOR IT?

When you contract with a professional for opinion polling services, you are paying for five things: the pollster's time and expertise in creating the questionnaire and analyzing the resulting data, his office overhead (and it almost always is *his* office), the sample he buys (i.e., the subset of people from a larger universe who are questioned), the price he pays to a professional interviewing service, and his data processing costs. The most elastic item on this list is the size and type of the sample. That controls the cost of interviewing.

Here's why. A sample composed simply of 500 otherwise unidentified county residents with telephones who are reached by random-digit dialing is very expensive. The reason is the number of "no hits" and call-backs the interviewers will encounter (phones that have been disconnected, only phone tape answering, no adult is home, respondent refuses to participate, etc.).

On the other hand, a random sample comprising 500 active voters in the library service area comes to the interviewing firm as a list of names and phone numbers drawn from a database compiled from the most recent election records of the appropriate county clerk. The hit rate, and the likelihood that the 500 interviews can be completed quickly and efficiently, is far greater—because active voters are less likely to move and marginally more willing to answer questions.

To go back to the original question: how much does a professional opinion poll cost? In Northern California in the fall of 1999, a 20-minute poll of 400 active voters cost $18,000. In Texas in 1998 the Westbank Library's poll cost $8,000. Polling consultant Gene Bregman of San Francisco says that prices tend to be regional and driven by competition inside the regional market. The polling markets on West and East coasts are highly competitive, which keeps prices lower, but that may not be the case in the Midwest and South.

Who pays for the opinion poll? This depends largely on your financial situation. Sometimes it is possible to get the powers that be (for example the city manager) to agree that the need for information is so critical it is worth spending regular library budget money to acquire it. Sometimes you can charge the cost of the poll to public relations, planning, or contracted services, satisfy the auditors, and hope to heaven that the opposition doesn't regard this as a golden opportunity to posture in the press about the misappropriation of the people's money.

Perhaps the key here is the sophistication and enthusiasm of the library's governance. If the board, or whoever, understands that without polling data there is little point in pursuing an election option, it will be more likely to approve use of the funds.

Often, however, it is the Friends of the Library or the nascent campaign committee that must come up with the money for the poll. And this is just as well, since the information gathered in the poll will be used for campaign strategic planning later on, and the data becomes the private property of the Friends.

Who pays for the poll brings up another question: who is the opinion pollster's client? This is important for all the standard reasons. Every project works better if one person has final responsibility and is therefore in charge of making final decisions. If the library is paying, then probably it is the library director who is the client, although it could be the board chair. If the Friends or the campaign committee are paying, it can be their president or chair.

There is, however, a reality to consider here. In most library campaigns, the library director plays an absolutely crucial role as organizer, thinker, and strategist, even if this work is done behind the scenes. So it may well be the best idea, regardless of who is paying, to declare the librarian the de facto client who works most closely with his or her professional colleague, the polling consultant.

But Do We Really Need to Hire a Professional?

The answer to that question is no, you don't, provided you have a lot of time, 20 to 30 volunteers, leadership and supervision from knowledgeable people, and access to data processing. These days there are even computer programs to help with data input and analysis. *Public Opinion Polling,*[1] by the Montana Alliance for Public Policy, was written specifically to help any citizen organization conduct its own perfectly valid opinion poll with very little cash expenditure.

The things you need to conduct your own opinion research are probably available to most library support organizations and may be easier to come by than the $10,000 to $20,000 needed for a professional poll. However, the critical issue could be time, not money. A group of 20 to 30 people working on conducting an opinion poll is expending energy and hours that might more profitably be spent on raising money for the campaign or visiting politicians. On the other hand, if the possibility of a tax election is a couple of years away, and you have the people and other requirements, doing your own poll might be a useful way to gather in and develop commitment among volunteers.

Information about how to do it yourself is widely available, so it will not be repeated here. Instead, let's focus on what never occurs to most of us until we do it the first time—contracting with a professional for an opinion polling project.[2]

Whom Do We Hire?

Assessing the technical competence of a potential polling consultant is the easy part. Does he or she have experience conducting polls of the sort you want (i.e., political polls as opposed to commercial market research)? Is he or she willing to submit sample reports from other jobs and references from other clients, especially like-situated clients?

It is enormously helpful if the polling consultant has done polls in your geographic area before and therefore has a working knowledge of its peculiarities (e.g., that the second district is a gerrymandered combination of farms and suburban sprawl). Most opinion polling consultants have regional practices.

The hard part of the selection process is finding someone to work with whom you like. The best way to do that is via an interview in which you assess the potential consultant's personal skills in the context of technical competence. Does he or she explain things without patronizing you? Does he or she have a stereotypical view of librarians? Worse, does he or she insist on telling you long stories about how he or she has always loved libraries? Do you instinctively trust the person's judgment? You are paying a lot of money for the services, so don't hire someone whose manners and style are going to drive you up the wall.

So where do you find this paragon of competence and charm? Well, certainly the correct advice would be to get recommendations from libraries that have conducted polls, to collect a few references from other agencies or elected officials, and then put out a request for quotations in letter format. But this is electoral politics, so here are two other approaches that may be more appropriate.

The first is standard advice you hear everywhere: ask your campaign consultant whom to hire for polling work. The reason is that the two of them will be working together very closely. The campaign consultant will have questions he or she particularly wants included in the poll. And as the days before the election count down, the consultant in the field may have specific queries for the pollster that will affect, for example, last-minute telephone targeting or a mailing to absentee voters. It helps if the pollster and the consultant trust one another's competence.

The problem with this advice is that it leaves out an important reality: many librarians and library supporters are hiring their first opinion pollster because they want to find out whether they should run a referendum or a ballot measure campaign. They are a long way from hiring a campaign consultant. So the best they can do to cover all bases is to ask potential pollsters which campaign consultants they typically work with and which kinds of campaigns they have been: local issues? state-wide issues? candidates?

Another tack is to ask your favorite elected official for advice. Who is his or her pollster, and what does the official think of their competence? Then ask the person for a meeting to discuss your needs.

In the political consulting and polling game, professionals tend to be Republicans or Democrats and to get most of their clients along party lines and through connections with campaign consultants. So a recommendation from your state senator is going to give you someone from her or his party who probably has never done a library poll but knows a lot about the political ins and outs of your county.

Party affiliation doesn't make any difference at all in the quality of the opinion poll conducted by the professional. It can, however, make a difference in your relationship with the pollster and the pollster's off-the-record comments about the data collected.

This ask-a-politician strategy worked well for the Santa Cruz City-County Library System, but see the nightmare scenario at the end of this chapter for another outcome.

WHAT DOES THE POLLING CONSULTANT DO?

The job of the polling professional is to conduct opinion research that answers the questions of the client. If the librarian is the only client, the pollster's task is probably easier. But in so many government and library situations, the person playing the client role is probably responsible to a variety of other people—the library board, the Friends board, an elected official, a city or county manager. All of these people may feel that they know as much about opinion polling as anyone else. And all of them may have strong ideas about how they think it should be conducted and what should be asked.

Finding ways to handle the inevitable problems that result from this kind of situation is one reason why picking a pollster who has worked satisfactorily for a successful local politician can be a real advantage. Such a person comes into the job with the imprimatur of someone who is known, and even people of the opposite political party tend to respect the judgment of the politician who won the election.

An added competency of any polling consultant has to be diplomatic skill. One of the pollster's jobs is to help the client weed through the contradictory advice she or he may be getting, explaining to a stubborn trustee why, for example, a particular type of question will not elicit the information desired.

Another task of the polling consultant is to help the client frame what the questions really are. "We want to know whether they'll vote for a tax increase," says the librarian or the campaign chair. "But what kind of tax increase, and how long should it last?" asks the pollster. "Also, have you thought about whether hooking up with the schools on the ballot would be a good idea?" The answers to these questions lead to setting the objectives of the poll.

The polling consultant then develops a draft questionnaire for review and comment by the client.[3] Professional interviewers subsequently test the questionnaire for time, difficulty of administration, and reliability. Here are some typical objectives for a preelection telephone poll:

• To assess the chances for passage by the voters of a measure to raise money for public libraries throughout Wishbone County by imposing one of the following taxes: a) a quarter-cent sales tax or b) a $0.68 per $100 increase in the property tax.

• To test whether the duration of either measure will increase the likelihood of passage.

• To determine voter attitudes and opinions toward the Wishbone County Library by testing how seriously respondents view current library problems, how important public libraries are to voters, and which services are most important to which voter groups.

This might be a poll of 400 randomly selected registered voters who speak English, and the resulting questionnaire might take 15 minutes to administer. Getting the interview time down to a reasonable level (15 to 18 minutes) wouldn't take much in a poll with such limited objectives, but the more you try to find out from a poll, the harder and longer it will be to administer.

LIBRARY POLL SAMPLES

All the textbooks on polling remind us to pay attention to who is being polled whenever we read a news account. When we gauge possible tax measure support, we are not interested in what the broad spectrum of county residents think, even if the broad spectrum is our library users. We need to know what the people who *vote* think

Table C

	Priorities				
	1	*2*	*3*	*4*	*5*
Opening all libraries six or seven days per week	39%	15%	16%	15%	16%
Improving collections and other services students for pre-schoolers, elementary and high school	22%	24%	16%	25%	14%
Repairing, maintaining, and improving Central Library	17%	24%	24%	25%	11%
Providing up-to-date computer technology and Internet access	12%	17%	14%	12%	46%
Repairing, maintaining, and improving your local branch library	11%	20%	31%	24%	15%

about it. In fact, our sample should probably be limited to *likely voters*—people who are registered to vote, voted in the last election, and are therefore likely to vote in the next one.

Here in California, likely voters are older, white, and have more money than the demographics of either the total state population or most individual counties. These people are not necessarily the heaviest public library users. But for the time being, what they think about public libraries and how they should be funded is far more important than anyone else's opinion because they are making the decision. We are not discussing what is right, but rather what is political reality.

Many pre–ballot measure polls not only gauge opinion about a new tax but also test which issues are most attractive to active voters, information that will be needed for the election campaign. Knowing that library open hours and services to children are the two highest priorities among county voters tells the campaign planners that the leaflets, the TV ads, and the standard pitch by the public speakers should all focus first on these issues. It means that the library director can go slow on trying to build pictures in the public mind of exciting new branches where neighborhoods have never had them before and start talking about family story hours when the central library and the existing branches are open on Sunday afternoon.

Remembering the limited nature of the sample is important in evaluating the results of these kinds of questions, of course, and it may help you understand some data that otherwise seem peculiar. For example, Table C is what Santa Cruz learned from a November 1995 poll about how voters would prioritize the spending of any new library tax money.[4]

It isn't the high ranking of open hours and services to kids that surprised us; we didn't need a poll to tell us those are the highest priorities, although it is useful to have the validation. No, instead look at the column on the far right. Forty-six percent of the respondents gave their *lowest* ranking to providing up-to-date computer technology and Internet access, which certainly didn't mesh with the enthusiastic walk-in response we had received to our public-access Internet workstations.

As I hastened to point out to our governing authorities at the time, however, the polling information was for use in mounting an effective election campaign. It was not a vote for or against a particular library service. In retrospect it is interesting to note how this data supported and presaged one of the most important conclusions of the Benton Foundation's *Buildings, Books and Bytes* research: people worry that in the digital age public libraries will not continue to provide books, which they see as important. They want a balance between books and technology.[5]

CONDUCTING THE POLL

Telephone opinion polls are conducted over a short time period—two to eight days depending on the sample size—so that the results are not skewed by a public event or news item that occurs in mid poll and affects the responses of a portion of the sample. The standards for speed are set by political candidates who want to know how they are doing at any given moment, but the need for quickness also applies to polls about public issues such as transportation planning or library tax measures.

Think about it: if half the sample is polled after a major hurricane devastates the county, that group's priorities for how tax money should be spent are going to be substantially different from those polled before the catastrophe.

Opinion pollsters contract with professional interviewing firms, who supply trained workers operating from facilities equipped with telephones and computers. These professional services work for many clients (pollsters) at the same time. They can provide data tabulation overnight.

One technique that can add cost but speeds up the interviewing process is computer-assisted interviewing (CATI). The interviewer sits at a video display terminal and keys responses directly into the computer. CATI is particularly helpful when the questionnaire is complicated by "skip pattern" queries (e.g., "If respondent says Yes, ask Question 5, if No, skip to Question 7").

The interviewing firm supplies "top line" results to the pollster (who later gives them to you) almost as soon as the interviews are completed. These are "frequency distributions" (how many people said yes or no to each question and the percent each number represents of the total sample).

The top-line data do not include subsets of information, such as the fact that it was the older voters with no children living at home who placed a low value on library computer services in the 1995 Santa Cruz poll. That kind of detail surfaces in the "cross tabulations," which are generated next.

Cross tabs look at answers to questions based on demographic data: gender, age, income group, residence, etc. Knowing that 52 percent of all respondents over age 65 would vote for a library tax but that the overall support level is 70 percent may tell you something useful about where you should or should not direct your campaign effort.

INTERPRETING THE POLL DATA

The responses must also be evaluated in terms of sampling error—a factor that the pollster will have calculated at the time the sample is drawn. A 5 percent margin of error means that there are 95 chances out of 100 that the poll is accurate. The error rate is used, among other things, to pick out which data from the poll are significant and which aren't. This is done by looking at any response rate by a subgroup that varies from the total by more than the error rate.

Suppose the error rate is 5 percent, and the total positive response to a tax for the library is 55 percent. Every subgroup total (men, women, voters in District 5) below 50 percent or above 60 percent is worth looking at to figure out why.[6]

It is the opinion pollster who goes through all the data with a fine-toothed comb, spotting aberrations and interesting anomalies. He or she analyzes the responses to each question and draws conclusions from the analysis. The pollster usually presents a draft, which gives you, the client, the opportunity to tell the pollster what you don't understand or to ask for more detailed analysis on a particular question.

Opinion poll reports are often presented with computer graphics showing details of responses. At a minimum the report should state the objectives of the poll, the methodology, the size and type of the sample, report results by question, and conclude with recommendations (e.g., "The annual cost of the tax measure should not exceed $26"). Both the questionnaire and the top-line results are attached as an appendix to the report.

Don't forget, too, to ask for the complete cross tabulations, even if you are mostly interested in reading the analytical report. You paid for them, and your campaign consultant may want them later.

Sometimes it is helpful also to ask the opinion pollster to produce a shorter "executive summary" report, which the library can use for broader distribution. It may be that you do not want either the press or the political opposition to have detailed access to your polling numbers on such issues as "most important library service," since this will telegraph your election campaign strategy long before it becomes obvious.

The pollster's conclusions may not be what you want to hear, of course. It is very hard to spend $10,000 or more on an opinion poll only to learn that you haven't a prayer of winning a tax election. Surely, though, you would rather know this ahead of time instead of after you have lost the election.

One reason to pay careful attention to the design of the questionnaire is so that at the end of the poll you at least know *why* the people won't support a library tax increase.

Focus Group Research

Focus groups, which collect qualitative data on how people feel or talk about issues, came into vogue for political campaigns in the 1980s. They were first developed by market researchers who wanted to gauge public support for new products or to frame advertising messages. These days the same consultants who do telephone polling usually provide focus group services.

A political focus group is a gathering of 6 to 12 individuals who talk in a relatively structured way about an issue or a candidate, aided by a moderator. Choosing the participants for the group depends on what the polling or campaign consultant is trying to discover. If, for example, the consultant wants to know the best message for a campaign literature piece aimed at senior citizens, obviously it is older people who need to be recruited for the group.

It is the consultant's task to ensure that the group includes a good sample of the target—in this case seniors who are likely to or can be persuaded to vote. The consultant will doubtless ask the client for help in recruiting participants, since the client is on the ground locally and knows the location of the mobile-home park with a big elderly population and which senior centers are most heavily used.

The moderator (or consultant) prepares 10 or so questions for discussion, starting with the general (to warm people up) and getting increasingly specific. What do seniors value

most about the library: novels in large print? medical and other self-help information? books and magazines they can't afford to buy? the weekly trip downtown?

The moderator works to keep the group discussion on track, taking careful notes of what is said and providing analysis of the notes afterwards. Often focus group sessions are videotaped, so the tape also becomes part of the analytical record.

Focus groups aren't "scientific," but as one pollster put it, "They give you a chance to hear how people *talk* about an issue." They are a useful method for validating and refining the information you collected using more statistically reliable quantitative methods.

Here's an example of a typical use of the focus group research methodology. In 1996 the Benton Foundation did a telephone opinion poll of 1,015 adults 18 or over, selected by random-digit dialing, to gauge public support for libraries in the digital age. The poll revealed some very interesting things. However, the Foundation wanted more detailed information about how people actually talk and think about libraries because it was trying to formulate new messages for librarians to use in explaining libraries. So the Foundation decided to follow up with a series of focus groups made up of library users in specific demographic categories.

The telephone poll had suggested that the public did not understand what librarians do and was ambivalent about what their role should be in the digital age. So the focus groups were asked to discuss how they think of librarians and—here's the crucial part—to react to the phrase "information navigator" as a role descriptor. Did the name make sense to the participants? The answer was yes. So the Benton Foundation has included it among the materials it is using (along with the Urban Libraries Council) to train librarians in new ways to talk to the public.[7]

It is practically impossible to say how much a focus group might cost because the price depends on what is being asked, how many groups are involved, the length of the discussion, and the amount of detail in the information being collected. Given that it is always better to overbudget than underbudget, plan on $5,000 at a minimum for three or four groups. Better,

however, would be leaving the whole matter to your campaign consultant, asking that firm to include research costs in the budget if focus groups will be required.

A final comment on focus groups: I understand the usefulness of focus groups in very large political campaigns—ones where the message on behalf of the issue or the candidate must be carefully calibrated for many different voter targets. But I do question whether the vast majority of library ballot measure campaigns need them. Intelligent campaign consultants are very good at looking at detailed quantitative data from a telephone poll, putting it together with other facts about the library, and formulating appealing campaign messages. If your campaign consultant wants to spend money on focus groups, be sure you understand why.

Read More About It

There are at least three good books, as well as a good article, on opinion polling. *Polling and the Public*, by Herbert Asher,[8] is a standard source now in its fourth edition. It is comprehensive in its treatment of the techniques and issues surrounding polling and pays particular attention to educating the public to be informed poll consumers. The chapter on elections could have spent a bit more time on ballot measures instead of candidates, but the basic principles are well covered.

Public Opinion Polling, by Celinda C. Lake, mentioned earlier, is basically a manual for citizen organizations (or libraries) that want to do their own polling because they can't afford to hire professionals. It covers everything from questionnaire design to interviewer training to coding the survey for data entry.

Jane Farley Templeton's *The Focus Group, a Strategic Guide to Organizing, Conducting, and Analyzing the Focus Group Interview*[9] is really about market research. However, it is interesting to translate the details of her information into political campaign terms.

Finally, William Hamilton, a Democratic pollster in Washington, D.C., takes us on a fascinating barefoot run through the history of the development of public and private political polling in a chapter of the book *Campaigns and Elections American Style*.[10]

A look at any of these sources will tell you everything you want or need to know about such topics as the use of screening questions, sampling techniques, the problem of "nonattitudes," impression-management, and weighting responses. These are interesting technical issues that apply to any poll conducted for anyone.

A Nightmare with a Happy Ending

Beth Wheeler Fox is the director of the Westbank Library outside of Austin, Texas.[11] Her library had always operated as a nonprofit library and managed to get pro bono help from attorneys and so forth whenever they needed it. Consequently, when the Westbank Library became Texas's first library district and prepared to go to the voters for funding, her board was extremely reluctant to cough up the $8,000 needed for a precampaign poll.

But in the end they conceded, and the library hired Texas's leading political polling firm. The company, obviously regarding the job as a standard toss off, sent an associate to do the poll. He turned out to be a self-described bookstore user who couldn't imagine why anyone would go to a library for

anything. In fact, his preconceptions were so strong that Fox and her staff found themselves asking each other, "Why are we dealing with *his* prejudices? We're trying to find out what the *public* thinks." They had to fight to get the right questions asked.

Truth, justice, and the American public library won in the end, however. Public support for the Westbank Library was extremely high (they later won their tax election by a whopping 84 percent), and the consultant went away commenting that his firm had never done a poll that had such a favorable rating for a public service. I wonder if he'll remember that next time he's in a megabookstore and can't find anything older than 1999 imprints.

4
Campaign Consultants

The conventional way to hire a campaign consultant is to ask around for suggested names, look up Political Consulting in the Yellow Pages or on the Internet, and match what you've heard with the names you find. You interview two or three and sign with the one who seems the most competent or seems competent enough and also offers your campaign a deal you can afford. Everything goes swimmingly up until election night, when losing is the consultant's fault or winning is because you and the other library supporters worked your bottoms off.

This is, of course, a somewhat jaundiced view of the typical relationship between library supporters and political campaign consultants. Some library groups, even ones that *lost* their ballot measure campaigns, continue to think the sun rises and sets in their consultants. And some others, who won, will never voluntarily speak to their consultants again.

Clear as mud, right? The relationship between a campaign consultant

and his or her clients can be very difficult, among other reasons because the interests of the two parties are so different.

The library support group wants to win. However, they're often not disciplined enough to do anything and everything the consultant asks in order to do so. The consultant says, "No, *don't* bother with yard signs; instead we should put our effort into telephoning." But one of the committee members, who also contributed $1,500 to the campaign, goes out and orders yard signs anyway and then co-opts six volunteers for installation work over the weekend the consultant wanted to blitz telephoning potential absentee voters.

The consultant wants to win too, but about 75 percent of her motivation (no matter what she says) is that she doesn't want to have a loss on her record (business is business, after all). The consultant is a professional who brings a lot of technical knowledge and skills to the campaign and would like to be respected (and trusted) for that. If she says no yard signs, there are good reasons why, and she thinks your job as the client is to, by golly, believe her.

One way to avoid problems in the client/consultant relationship is to have clear expectations of each other, to have those expectations written down, and to be sure there are mechanisms built into the contract document for enforcement. It is very easy, in the last hectic weeks before election day, to let agreements slide, only to find yourself in an argument later about who did or said what and who is going to pay the bill for it. So let's look at developing the relationship part by part.

Do You Need a Campaign Consultant?

The quick answer to this question is no, you don't, not if you don't mind losing. But if you want to win, and you have any opposition at all, you would be very wise to hire a pro to help.

It is not easy to persuade 50 percent plus one (let alone 66.6 percent) of voters to approve a tax increase, no matter how popular the library is. In fact, it is much easier to persuade 50 percent plus one of the voters to say no to a tax increase—even if they are library users.

A professional brings a campaign the ability to look at polling data and develop strategy and tactics from them; solid knowledge about targeting and the computer programs to do that work efficiently; expertise in preparing campaign literature pieces; and a lot of experience in fund-raising, managing volunteers, and dealing competently with the inevitable last-minute crises.

The professional's advice and opinions are based on documented experience in other campaigns—not on the rosy memories of what worked when a campaign committee member was helping elect Senator So-and-So or fighting the Crosstown Expressway.

You could, of course, teach yourself to do the things a campaign consultant does. Indeed, the next chapter spends some pages describing the nuts and bolts of targeting, although the purpose is to convey how important this technique is to devising campaign strategy.

If you are the library director, however, you don't have time to do what the consultant will do, unless you take a year-long leave of absence to attend campaign training institutes and then run the campaign. And if you are a library supporter, the same applies, even if you are retired and think you can devote full time to the election.

Professional campaign consultants bring one other thing to the process, which is probably their most essential contribution: they *love* the electoral process and they *love* campaigns. Consultants are deeply and sincerely interested in what motivates tiny demographic sectors of the populace to vote yes or no on issues, and they are willing to spend hours thinking about how to persuade them. Are you? No, you aren't. You want to win and get on with delivering information services to the library's constituents. So, if at all possible, hire a professional to help so you can.

How Much Does a Consultant Cost?

Campaign consultant fees vary regionally but probably are about 30 percent to as much as 40 percent of the total campaign budget. So if the consensus of local opinion is that it is going to take $100,000 to win Measure G, expect to spend a minimum of $25,000 on the campaign consultant, plus another $10,000 as a winning bonus.

The consultants who favor the winning bonus option say it conveys their confidence in their own track record and rewards them for a job well done. Those who don't, believe their professionalism demands a flat payment win or lose. Whatever, comparing prices among consultants, you will probably end up paying roughly the same amount no matter which type you hire.

Whom to Hire

Campaign consultants tend to have regional practices, and they are usually associated with one or another of the political parties. Some specialize in issue campaigns and others in candidates. In my home state of California one or two consultants have developed subspecialties in library campaigns because there have been so many. And a few offer multiple services: opinion polling, public relations, and lobbying, as well as campaign management.

I suspect that word of mouth is the most common way of developing a consultant short list. Librarians and library groups tell one another whom they hired and whether they liked them. Occasionally a local elected official will make a strong recommendation, although it is important to evaluate whether the consultant in question is good because he got the official elected, or because he or she also has experience with issue campaigns.

Another person to ask is your opinion pollster if you have one. Many polling professionals work closely with campaign consultants and have good ideas about who would work well in your community or with your library group.

There is also the buzz factor. A consultant emerges out of the crowd to win a surprise victory, and suddenly candidates or groups all over the region are lining up to hire her.

Whatever the means, develop a short list of three or four candidates, and write a letter to each requesting proposals by a certain date. The letter should give the consultant the basic facts: what will be on the ballot when, why you need the money, and how much, preliminarily, you are thinking of spending on the campaign. Make it clear that you want strategic planning services from the consultant, so none of your current plans (including how much money you plan to raise) are hard and fast.

This last point is important because no support group ever plans to raise what will really be needed. Consultants know that part of their job is bringing the campaign the bad news about the total budget required. Ask the consultant candidate to submit a letter of interest, including fees, a statement of experience, a list of former-client references, and a sample contract.

Notice that you are *not* asking the consultant to speculate about a campaign plan in his or her proposal. If the consultant offers this advice up front it can only be for two reasons: he knows your area and its demographics very well because he has worked there quite recently on a comparable issue, or he is exploiting his reputation as the hottest thing in campaign consulting since automated voter registration files. He won in X with such-and-such

a strategy, and trust him, it will work for YOU. He might be right, but watch out anyway.

Invite the most likely respondents to come to town for an interview, and plan to spend at least an hour talking with each of them about your campaign. The candidates ought to have a detailed list of questions to ask you— some of which will be embarrassing, such as how much money have you raised so far ("Uh, well, actually, not very much"), let's see your polling data, and what makes you think you can win?

The potential campaign consultant wants to know whether she or he is dealing with probable losers or potential winners, just as you want to know whether this alien from a different world is really someone with whom you can work. Try not to be dazzled by the consultant's jargon.

If the consultant has provided what you asked for in your letter (especially samples of previous work and references to former clients), your questions should focus on getting a sense of the consultant's work style and office organization. How many other clients will the consultant be handling in the coming election? How many professionals and other staff are in his office? How many hours would the consultant devote to you and your campaign, and to whom would he assign the rest of the work?

The normal pattern is for the firm's principal to think about and okay the overall strategy and for "associates" to manage the daily work. The question is, are there enough associates? Also, do you like the one assigned to you, and what are his or her qualifications? A clever consultant will have brought the likely associate to the interview.

All campaigns have crisis moments in the final days in which everyone from the consultant's staff to the local committee is working flat out 18 hours per day. But if the consultant's staff is going to be so busy with so many clients that it is operating in crisis mode 10 weeks out from election day, you need to think carefully about whether you want to hire these people.

It is hard to make this judgment when you don't really know the details of the campaign consulting business, but try to apply logic. Does your common sense tell you that a principal and one associate, plus three secretaries, are enough people to handle 25 campaigns all at once?

You can get some help answering that question by calling up the consultant's previous client references. First, make sure you are talking with the person who did the real campaign work, not just the titular co-chair. Then ask a whole series of nitty-gritty questions: did the consultant do what he said he would do? Did she stay on schedule and on budget? Could you get through to him on the phone when you called,

or was it always a promised call back that often didn't come?

Did the people in her office treat you with respect? Could they answer simple questions? Were the consultant's subcontractors (the graphic artist, the printer, the mail house) accessible or rude? Did your informant like the consultant, and perhaps more important, did she or he like the people who work for him?

If all these questions sound unnecessarily picky, consider this: sometimes campaign consultants make their reputations on strokes of absolute brilliance—the fantastic ad that drew the winning margin to the polls or the strategy that produced a 75 percent yes vote where a tax measure had never before won. The trouble is the price the client can sometimes pay for that brilliance: office disorganization, seat-of-the-pants decision making, and every single campaign task, from getting the volunteer sign-up cards to the printer to drafting the ballot Argument in Favor, done at the last minute.

By no means does every really smart consultant operate this way. But some do, and you surely want to know in advance if you are hiring one. The hassle could be worth it to you. Or maybe, with an advance alert, these are problems you could fix in the contract.

The Consultant Contract

Campaign consultants have standard service contracts that they expect their clients to sign. Typically, the contracts specify the following:

• The services to be performed (e.g., planning the political strategy, devising a budget, directing the field campaign, selecting the vendors for and overseeing the preparation of campaign literature, media pieces, etc.).

• The fees for the service, and the time schedule for paying (e.g., 10 percent on signing and the balance by a date the week before the election).

• Other campaign costs and vendor payment procedures. The consultant isn't responsible for paying the printer or the mail house, even though he or she is supervising them. The contract will specify this, as well as stating clearly that the consultant won't *advance* any vendor fees either. You will find out just how important this standard clause is the day your campaign committee chair or treasurer gets a phone call from the mail house saying that it will not release your 30,000-piece mailing (which was due to go out yesterday) until you turn up with a check for $2,500. Oh, and make that a certified check, please, because we've dealt with campaigns before.

• The procedures for hiring and paying campaign staff, if any, to run the field operation. Again, the cost for such staff is not included in the consultant fee.

• Procedures for reimbursing the consultant's travel, phone calls, hotel, and other expenses.

• Due diligence, warranty, indemnification, waiver, termination, late payment, and other boilerplate clauses. These are worth reading carefully, in case you get into an argument or forget something later. For example, the consultant's contract might stipulate that the designs of the campaign products (the leaflets, bumper stickers, and so forth) are the property of the consultant. However, the voter tapes, files, and lists (which the campaign committee paid for separately) are jointly owned. The consultant will have used these tapes and lists on his or her office computer and therefore probably kept them. But since they are joint property, you might want to ask for them later for some library use.

There are two important things you can do with a standard campaign consultant contract for services. The first is to ask for changes in the details (such as the payment terms) if you want them. The consultant is in business and of course wants the best deal he or she can make with clients. But if the treasurer fears out-of-pocket expense charges for penthouse suites and rented limousines, put in a monthly cap clause. Actually, most consultants don't have time for penthouse suites or luxury cars, but you're the customer, so go for what will make your campaign treasurer feel better.

The second thing to do is to require an addendum to the contract, to be completed by a date certain (say one month after signing), which sets out the campaign schedule, deadlines, and budget for both the consultant and the campaign committee. The next chapter will discuss the campaign calendar in more depth. Suffice it to point out here that after formulating the campaign strategy, one of the most important consultant tasks is to set up a calendar of campaign events.

This calendar drives the activities that go into making the events happen. If October 12 is the Saturday the yard signs start going up, then they must be delivered by the previous Wednesday. Yard-sign copy should therefore have gone to the sign maker by September 6, and so forth.

The point about a fairly precise calendar is that it can save lots of argument later. It provides a guide to who is supposed to be doing what when, as well as how much money is going to be needed by what date—$3,000 to the contractor for the yard signs on October 9 for example.

A detailed calendar also gives you the chance to look at the proposed work flow and manipulate it. Yard signs, to

stick with the example, are not rocket science. They have a clear, short message, and are printed in appallingly bright colors such as fluorescent pink and black. There isn't a reason in the world (except lack of cash) why they can't go to the maker in July, when the shop isn't so busy, instead of waiting for the big rush in September.

Now the consultant may argue that this kind of scheduling detail is his or her responsibility, not the campaign committee's, and that anyway, "electoral politics don't work that way." Campaigns must remain flexible and able to respond quickly in the face of crises. The committee should argue back that careful, detailed scheduling is to everyone's advantage: it makes expectations clear, and makes it easier to respond to last-minute events.

I am sure that fully half the problems clients have with consultants, and that consultants have with clients, would be solved if the two agreed on that detailed schedule and then made every possible effort to stick to it.

Money and the Campaign Budget

The other common area of potential client-consultant conflict is the campaign budget. Probably the consultant's standard contract will specify that once the budget has been set, it will take written notice by the client to cancel or change it.

This makes sense from the consultant's point of view: he doesn't want

to have to stop to negotiate with the committee on the price of printing a leaflet in the middle of a hot campaign. He needs to know that $5,000 has been budgeted for getting out this literature piece and that how that money is divided between the graphic artist, the printer, and the mail house is up to him.

But from the campaign committee's perspective, what's to stop the consultant from going over budget on some item and then expecting the client to pay the bill? Surely it would be reasonable (and common sense) for the campaign committee to require a contract clause that refers to the campaign budget and sets up a mechanism for ensuring that it is followed. For example, the budget might specify an "amount not to exceed" for an activity, and the contract could require that the consultant (after a balancing process at the end) pay the difference if the item goes over budget.

Consultants seem to believe (based on their experience, of course) that money is not as important as winning and that the campaign committee will be able to raise what is needed in the end. And to an extent they are right. It is true that the committee chair can get on the phone and raise a quick $2,000 to cover the printing bill if it is really, really needed, and the campaign feels like it is going to win. The

chair can do this, the consultant will point out, because people vastly prefer to give money to specific things instead of general budgets. Those parties and fund-raisers political candidates always have to "pay off the campaign debt" are just this sort of activity after the fact.

We library people have trouble with this kind of thinking because we are so used to struggling to make ends meet. Most library directors would no more overspend their annual budgets than they would take off for Acapulco with yesterday's overdue fines (not that fine revenue would get them much further than the airport). This flexibility and somewhat cavalier attitude about money is an important cultural difference between library clients and their campaign consultants.

My conviction is that the best way to handle it is to build mechanisms for sticking to the budget into the contract and be prepared to try to be flexible as time marches down to election day.

A Consulting Nightmare

"You're not going to believe this," said Marty Taylor as she burst into Library Director Vanessa Woods's office on the Wednesday afternoon six days out from the election. "Doyle L. has done it to us again. Look at this," and she slapped a copy of a campaign mail piece on Woods's desk.

"Oh no!" said Woods, staring at it. The piece had a nice photograph of

one of the library branches, and the headline "If Measure L Passes the Fairview Memorial Library Will Stay Open!"

"Fairview MEMORIAL Library? Memorial to what? That isn't its name. Those *fools*! We're going to be the laughing stock of all of Fairview. We don't even know the name of our own library. Aren't there any proofreaders or fact checkers at Doyle L.?" Doyle Lonnegan Associates was the campaign consulting firm under contract to the library, which had a major tax measure on the ballot.

"Well brace yourself, because it gets worse. They've used the same headline on the pieces about the Downtown and North Forty branches."

"Oh they couldn't have. I told them specifically they could *not* use that slogan for Downtown and North Forty because even if we lose there is *no way* we are going to close those branches. We talked about it at least twice. Sure it's a good slogan, but we *can't* lie to people, threatening to close branches that aren't in danger. And I was really clear about that to Doyle L."

"Well, I guess he didn't hear you. Or if he did, he decided to go with it anyway. Of course, he doesn't have to live here after the election," said Marty, who was a Friends member working full time for the campaign. "I called Doyle L. this morning to complain but, as usual, got put on hold. I don't suppose there's anything to be done anyway. If I ever get through to him, I'm going to read him the riot act. This is the last straw!"

"Well, I hope you give it to him in spades. But meanwhile, I think I should call Mike at Fairview. We need to work out how he handles it. It wouldn't be smart to blame the consultant, I guess. How about a line like, 'Yes, I saw it. Isn't that funny? A memorial to whom, I wonder? I am so glad this happened in Fairview though, because here everyone knows the name of their library.' What do you think? We should probably just lie low

on the Downtown and North Forty leaflets and hope nobody notices."

A head appeared in the doorway. "Hi!" said Janie Farnsworth, of the office staff. "Are you ready for some late-breaking news on the election front?"

"No!" said Marty and Vanessa in one voice.

"Trust me, you're going to love this. I just heard it on WXZZ, and I quote, Bobby Rice, frontrunner in the race for state assemblyman, was arrested by sheriff's deputies this morning for cultivating marijuana in his garage. Can you believe it? That supercilious fake; did I ever tell you about the time he came on to me at a party? I gather he had a hydroponic growing operation, with lights and tubes and the whole thing."

"Well there's this," said Vanessa with a sigh. "Bobby should keep the library off the front pages until next Tuesday. Poor guy. I wonder who put the sheriff on to him?"

If this library were alone on the ballot in a low-turnout or special election, the consultant's use of a slogan that distorts facts could mean serious trouble at the polls. Fortunately, there were other ballot measures and candidates running for office. Generally speaking, candidates (even ones who don't grow marijuana in their garages) can be relied on to create enough excitement in the final days of a campaign to distract attention from the library.

As for the consultant's use of a slogan that the library director had specifically vetoed, it is probably another example of the basic cultural difference between the two.

As Taylor points out, she and Woods have to live there after the election. Doyle L.'s principal concern is winning, and while he wouldn't break the law to do so, he might certainly play fast and loose with a client's preferences. Did Woods put her instruction about the slogan in writing? She should have.

As for getting the name of one of the branch libraries wrong, this is the kind of infuriating mistake that happens. I heard once about a library that had 3,000 buttons printed with the slogan, "Vote Yes for Libaries!" They used them, and they won.

5

Strategy: Part One of the Campaign Plan

Back in eighteenth-century New England, if Ebenezer Pomfret wanted the 75-member town meeting to vote in favor of letting him build a gristmill at the creek falls on town property, he'd spend several Saturdays visiting his neighbors, make sure to talk to friends at church, and stand by the door on town meeting day. His message would be targeted to the interests of his voters: End those long wagon trips to Hadley! Vote yes for a local place to grind our grain! And he'd manage to buttonhole and talk with every one of them.

Well, that was then and this is now. And now it is absolutely impossible, even with television, to reach every voter with a message. So campaigns make decisions—they devise a strategy—about where to put the campaign's resources: its people, time, and money.

Strategy is a combination of *whom* you want to vote for your measure and the reasons you tell them they should do so. As political consultant Allan Hoffenblum[1] put it so succinctly, Who + Why = 50 percent plus one (or for a California tax measure, 66.6 percent). *How* the campaign reaches the voters with its message (standing by the meeting room door? canvassing? direct mail?) are the tactics.

This strategy is one part of the overall campaign plan. The other two parts are the campaign budget and the calendar, which are discussed in the next chapter.

Establishing the Who

Do you remember how your ninth-grade English teacher was always talking about "narrowing the topic"? You wanted to write about "The Environment" and she suggested that perhaps a better subject might be "Pollution of the Housatonic River."

Establishing the who is basically "narrowing the topic." First, it is estimating which voters are likely to vote in the upcoming election. Then you figure out which ones are highly likely to vote yes on your measure (*your base vote*), which ones might vote yes if presented with the right arguments to do so (*the swing vote*), and finally, which voters aren't worth spending campaign resources on because they will never be persuaded to vote yes (the *opposition's base vote*).

HOW MANY PEOPLE MIGHT VOTE AND WHO ARE THEY?

Answering this question gives the campaign Fact Number One—the most important piece of information it needs: *how many votes it will take to win*. If turnout in the 1998 November election was 41,796, and if you expect it to be roughly the same in 2002, and you need 50 percent plus one to win, that is 20,899 votes, minimum. It is helpful to know this number so that you can think tactically about how you are going to get that many votes.

The campaign establishes this number by looking at previous comparable election data and by evaluating

what else is going to be on the ballot. The word *comparable* is crucial here. If your tax measure will be on the ballot in a low-turnout election, your campaign needs to work with the data from a previous low-turnout year, comparing apples and apples, not apples and oranges.

Different people vote in low-turnout elections—primarily, those who are absolutely convinced of the rightness or wrongness of the issue on the ballot. Most other people stay home. High-turnout elections, when there are national and state-wide candidates on the ballot, draw a much broader and quite different spectrum of voters.

You know, simply from a perusal of the district registration statistics, how many voters are Democrats, Republicans, Independents, and so forth. The issue is, how likely are they to vote in the next election?

The local elections commission can help answer this question by selling the campaign computerized data showing the voting performance over the past two or three elections of every voter in the district. This isn't information about *how* individually they voted; it is only whether or not they turned up at the polls or filed an absentee ballot. An opinion-polling consultant, doing a poll of, say, 500 likely voters, buys one of these tapes and uses it to randomly select voters for his statistical sample.

Suppose that the last election comparable to the one you are facing occurred in 1998. There was a reasonably big turnout (65 percent overall) because the governor was running for reelection, but also on the ballot was a local bond measure to build the desperately needed new high school. Equating interest in the school bonds to interest in the proposed library measure could lead you to conclude that turnout in 2002 should be about the same.

However, there is a possible ringer here. The pro–gun control folks are circulating a petition to place a statewide initiative on the ballot banning all handgun sales. And rumor has it that their signature collection effort is going very well. This means that the whole 2002 election could well be skewed by a loud and messy debate about handguns, with both sides working to turn out their partisans. So predicted turnout could jump to 75 percent (24,114 votes needed to win), with some of those voters being people who might not support the library.

WHO ARE THE LIBRARY'S VOTERS AND WHERE DO THEY LIVE?

The opinion poll provides the most useful data about who is likely to vote for the library measure. Look carefully at the demographic and other information in the cross tabulations (see chapter 3). Are the people who most strongly support the library (and are therefore the likely Yes voters) Democratic and Republican women of all ages for instance, plus Democratic men between 30 and 50? Which groups provided the lowest support? Repub-

lican men over age 50? University students who are renters? And so forth.

With this information in hand the campaign can go on to look at how strong Republican voter registration is and how the Republicans did in the last general election. Which precincts did the Republican candidate for governor win, even though he lost this district? Partisan information is important (even if public libraries are not a partisan issue) because of who will be drawn to the polls. Winning the library measure in the middle of a hot contest over gun control will require a different strategy than if the incumbent governor's reelection is a slam-dunk.

Now let's go back and look a little more closely at that 1998 election. The school bonds passed but by less than 1,500 votes. In District 3, which is one of the eight areas where your measure will be running, there was a 63 percent turnout of the 7,630 registered voters. Table D shows the data from the ten precincts: total registered voters in the precinct, the total who voted, and the voter "performance," i.e., the votes cast as a percent of the precinct's total registered voters.

Column E shows the "% Effort." This measures the percent of the total District 3 vote contributed by the precinct. So it is that Precinct Seven, which turned out only 54 percent of its registered voters, nevertheless contributed 10 percent of the total votes cast.

Precinct Seven is therefore more important statistically than Precincts One, Three, Four, and Ten but less important than Two, Five, Eight, and the others with more than 10 percent.

Table D

District 3, 1998

A Precinct	B Total Regist.	C Votes Cast	D Performance	E % Effort	F Yes	G No
ONE	467	254	54%	5%	100	154
TWO	908	595	66%	12%	466	129
THREE	308	237	77%	5%	175	62
FOUR	742	392	53%	8%	165	227
FIVE	1,097	713	65%	15%	360	353
SIX	772	520	67%	11%	265	255
SEVEN	906	490	54%	10%	260	230
EIGHT	979	698	71%	15%	398	300
NINE	863	525	61%	11%	375	150
TEN	588	382	65%	5%	125	257
TOTALS	7,630	4,806	63%		2,689	2,117

That means that if later you decide that a good tactic is precinct walking, and you haven't the resources to walk every precinct, you start at the top with the precincts with the highest turnout: Five and Eight.

Now look at the Yes and No votes for the school bonds. The bonds carried in District 3 with 56 percent of the vote. Indeed, the 572-vote victory contributed substantially to the overall win. But the bonds lost in Precincts One, Four, and Ten.

There are two things worth noting about these precincts. First, they only accounted for a collective 18 percent of the total vote (Column E). This means there may be strong antipathy to school bonds in these locations but not enough voters there to carry an election, especially with a turnout of less than 55 percent in two of the precincts.

Second, the precincts in question are, as it happens, dominated by three

mobile home parks housing a large group of poorer people and elderly citizens on fixed incomes (Precinct One), an assisted-living seniors' housing complex (Precinct Four), and the district's wealthiest subdivision (Precinct Ten). Most of these voters can be expected to oppose any kind of tax measure but especially one that builds a fancy new high school for someone else's kids.

So the question becomes, if they opposed the school bonds, will they also oppose our library measure? The answer might be "maybe not" because the bookmobile makes heavily used stops at the trailer parks. But if they do oppose us, will it matter?

Next, on the assumption that most people who voted for a school bond measure in 1998 will vote for a library measure in 2002, identify your "base" vote—the precincts that produced substantial majorities for the school bonds. The most important of these will be the ones that also accounted for more than 10 percent of the total vote: Precincts Two and Nine. It is nice that the bonds won 175 to 62 in Precinct Three, but with only 5 percent of the total vote the victory there wasn't vital.

Among other things, knowing where your base is gives you information for election day. You may not have to do much to persuade them to vote yes for the library, but getting these voters to the polls will be critical.

On the other hand, the precincts where the vote was close (Precincts Five, Six, Seven, and Eight) may well require special campaign efforts. These are particularly important because they also accounted for 51 percent of the total votes cast. The Yes margin there (145 votes) is close enough to lead the campaign committee to give some careful thought to the kind of effort it will make in those precincts.

And don't forget that your swing vote is also the opposition's swing. If the antilibrary-tax people mount a strong campaign they will probably target Five, Six, Seven, and Eight as precincts, which can potentially be organized to vote no on the library measure. The voting residents of these neighborhoods may find themselves the most popular people in District 3 by election day.

A lot of this data gathering and analysis is work that can and should be done by or with the help of the campaign consultant. She has the expertise for such tasks as acquiring the tapes from the local election commission, running them on her house computer, and correlating them with the data provided by the opinion poll. It is important to understand the principles, however, if for no other reason than that it never hurts to know what you are paying your campaign consultant to do.

Establishing the Campaign Why

The second element of the campaign strategy is the Why. This is *not* simply the reason the library and its supporters placed a tax measure on the ballot (because the library needs more operating funds or a new building). Rather, it is the reason why people should vote yes for the measure: because their kids or grandchildren love libraries, or because the South Fork Branch will close if they don't.

The Why message is an appeal to the voter's self-interest. It is established by taking a very careful look at the Who, making an educated guess as to what the interests of the Who are, and combining or verifying that with the information gathered in the opinion poll.

Here's an example. Suppose your base vote comprises Republican and Democratic women of all ages and your opinion poll tells you that 70 percent of the likely voters rate the quality of public education and cutbacks in library service as the area's most serious problems. Even the least imaginative campaign consultant would probably conclude from this data that the Why message should be built around library services to children, with a strong link to education.

A lot of the decision about devising and conveying the Why message rests on the local situation. If the area is enormous—voters spread over thousands of square miles, with little to unite them but their general feeling that they aren't getting what they pay for from their tax dollars—the campaign might go for general themes that dissociate libraries from government.

Or suppose the town is brand new—a bedroom community that has tripled in size in the last decade and is playing infrastructure catch-up. Then the strategy might be built around getting voters where they shop on weekends (since they aren't home in the daytime), and the message might be built around the needs of kids (could they be at the library after school?) and what any decent American community should provide.

Ample polling data support the contention that most voters know remarkably little about how their government really works and virtually nothing about the reality of government finance. So it is that they look at the North Forty Branch and believe that it stands alone. It is "their" local library, and never mind that its operating funds come from the county or a library district, although it is surely gross discrimination by the county government if North Forty's open hours are cut.

At least one consultant has built several winning campaigns around the theory that people will vote for a county-wide tax measure if they can be persuaded to see it in terms of their own local library.[2] So the strategy becomes a message based on polling data about the interests of library voters (the education of their children) couched in terms of the needs of the branch library where the voter lives.

In Santa Cruz in 1996 consultant Larry Tramatola and Associates did targeted mailings to the voters in the precincts surrounding each of the library system's nine branches. The front of the primary literature piece featured the photograph of an attractive white-haired woman reading to a small girl, with the slogan, "Nothing gives me greater joy than reading to my granddaughter at the library. Please vote YES on Measure B to save our library."

The piece opened out to a picture of a library branch, specific information about the needs of that branch, and two more key campaign messages: "If Measure B passes, our library will stay open," and "Measure B is not a Tax Increase" (it was a continuation of an existing tax about to expire). On the back was a "partial list" of some 1,000 endorsers surrounding a copy of the *San Jose Mercury News* editorial supporting the measure.

The Santa Cruz campaign spent a lot of money on mailings, a subject to which we will return in chapter 9. But the strategy of targeting the voters based on their likely loyalty to neighborhood branch libraries could have been implemented using other tactics. For example, campaign volunteers might have gone door-to-door talking about restoring open hours at the Boulder Creek Branch or expanding the parking lot at Aptos. For the price of pizza and soda young Friends on bicycles could have been deployed to distribute special campaign leaflets at every house in every neighborhood. Or telephone banks might have been organized around putative branch use. Usually, the amount of money raised or the number of volunteers available determines which tactics will be used.

Another popular campaign strategy is to build the campaign around constituencies (e.g., library user groups or supporters). Using the campaign's overarching themes ("We owe it to our children" or whatever), plus messages tailored to the interests of the targeted groups, the campaign organizes speeches, mailings, and phone calls to persuade teachers, union members, or the membership of the Save Our River Alliance to support the measure.

This strategy can be particularly effective if the library supporters have managed to negotiate coalitions with other groups—we'll support your measure next year if you'll support ours now. The wealthiest campaigns can devise different messages for different constituencies—business groups, parent-teacher organizations, etc.

On the matter of targeting library users, let's go back to Table C, which shows the District 3 school bond vote in 1998. Remember precincts One and Four, which both voted against the measure? Their voters mostly live in mobile homes and a senior housing complex. Up until last year the library's bookmobile made several stops in this area, and that service halted only when the vehicle died after 25 years on the

road. At $140,000, a new bookmobile isn't in the cards until the library measure passes.

Here's an obvious opportunity to devise a unique message for a special group of voters who, even though they may putatively be the opposition's base, could possibly be convinced to vote for the library. The most effective tactic might well be door-to-door canvassing by a mobile-home-park resident.

But there is another important thing to remember about precincts One and Four: they are small and probably not worth a substantial effort. If the library director's mother or a dedicated Friend is a resident of the assisted-living seniors' community and wants an assignment, by all means send her out with a stack of leaflets. But the whole point of devising a campaign strategy is to decide on the primary voter targets and the message to convey.

Successful campaigns agree on a strategy and are disciplined enough to stick to it. They do not allow themselves to be seduced by the opportunity to pick up a few votes here, when a major group of voters are waiting for the message over there.

The other two parts of the campaign plan—the budget and the calendar—are largely determined by the strategy. If the campaign committee has decided that staffing literature tables outside the library branches and getting "Vote Yes on Measure L" onto the Republican Party's election day door hangers is enough to win, there won't be much money to raise or time-planning to do. If the committee thinks the campaign may take more, however, read the next chapter.

Adding Up and Counting Backward: The Budget and the Calendar

Now that the campaign committee knows who it is aiming to persuade to vote yes for the library measure, and has agreed on what the message will be, it can develop the other two elements of the campaign plan: the budget and the calendar. The budget is needed so the committee knows how much money it has to raise, and the calendar—among other things—provides deadlines by which the dollars must be available.

The budgeting part can be depressing, especially if it turns out that far more money than you thought will be required to win. On the other hand, devising the calendar is invigorating because it makes the whole process of mounting a campaign look real and doable.

Devising a Campaign Budget

One way to approximate a campaign budget is to ask around the community and find out what other groups have raised and spent for other measures. How much did it take to win that water fluoridation initiative last year or the school bond election?

Of course it is necessary to think about the comparability of the election issues because it takes different amounts of effort and money to win different kinds of campaigns. Public libraries ought to be a bit less controversial than water fluoridation. On the other hand, while many voters automatically approve money for school or library buildings, they may be loath to agree to new operating funds for any government agency.

At any rate, call up the people who were on the committees, and ask what their campaigns cost and what they spent the money on. And while you're at it, don't forget to ask if they'll share their donor lists.

Suppose you learn that the school bond campaign raised and spent $60,000. But you realize that the school district is smaller than the library service area, so you up your best guess as to how much your campaign will need by another $20,000 to cover the added territory. Also, there was practically no opposition to the school bond measure, whereas you know that the anti-tax folks are warming up for a major assault on the library's proposed sales tax.

Based on information from the water fluoridation people (who faced well-financed opponents), you guess that fighting the opposition might take another $15,000 (for newspaper ads and an extra mailing). This brings your budget up to $95,000.

Even though these are merely approximate figures (precision will come later), you can now use the work you did on developing a campaign strategy to divide the money among the campaign elements. Suppose the committee and the consultant have agreed that the strategy will be to target regions of the library service area with special mailings and that the campaign will make a concentrated effort to go after absentee voters. The effort will include

a lot of telephone contacts, and it will use yard signs because local tradition demands them. The campaign won't bother with television or radio ads (relying instead on free interview shows) because the media market is much bigger than the library service area. The consultant believes newspaper advertising is not nearly as effective as direct mail but agrees to one major ad in the last week before the election if there is enough money left at that point. Finally, the campaign will set aside some funds for Get Out the Vote (GOTV) activities.

Those are the costs for things that directly reach the voters. But of course a campaign has a lot of other expenses. First and probably biggest in the "other" category is the campaign consultant. Then—unless there are donated space and competent volunteers—there is the office, clerical help, and a field manager who runs the day-to-day operations, such as coordinating volunteers and finding a dry place to temporarily store 500 yard signs. It costs money to raise money, so funds must be budgeted for mailings and other special events. The consultant will probably want to spend money for last-minute runs of computerized address and phone lists for absentee voters and the like—expenses that can be lumped together as "research." Finally, don't forget to budget for feeding the volunteers and the victory party on election night.

Table E sets out a fairly detailed campaign budget and adds some information about where the money might come from. Obviously, this is a pretty important speculation. Campaigns have two kinds of financial

Table E
Sample Campaign Budget

	COST	CASH	IN-KIND
PRINT LITERATURE			
Fund-raising Letter/Reply Cards, Envelopes	3,500.00	3,500.00	
Regional Target Mailing Pieces × 4	17,500.00	17,500.00	
Absentee Jumbo Postcard	4,000.00	4,000.00	
Miscellaneous Printing/Copying	1,000.00	1,000.00	
GOTV Door Hanger Share	1,500.00	1,500.00	
POSTAGE & MAIL HOUSE SERVICES			
Fund-raising Mailing	950.00	950.00	
Regional Target/Absentee Mailings	12,500.00	12,500.00	
ADVERTISING			
Newspaper Ad, 2 Days Out	600.00	600.00	
Yard Signs, 2 Color, 2 Face × 500, Sticks	5,000.00	5,000.00	
Vote Yes for Libraries Buttons	750.00	750.00	
Vote Yes for Libraries Bumper Stickers	1,500.00	1,500.00	
PERSONNEL			
Campaign Consultant	30,000.00	30,000.00	
Field Manager @ $600/week × 12	7,200.00	7,200.00	
Graphic Artist (Design/Layout All Pieces)	3,000.00	3,000.00	
Photographer (Target Mailing Piece)	120.00	120.00	
Travel/Out-of-Pocket Expenses	900.00	900.00	
RESEARCH COSTS			
County Clerk Tapes, Other Data	650.00	650.00	
HEADQUARTERS SPACE			
Rent @ $750/month × 3	2,100.00		2,100.00
Phones @ $50/month × 3	150.00		150.00
Utilities @ $150/month × 3	450.00		450.00
Supplies	200.00	200.00	
Insurance @ $30/month × 3	90.00		90.00
Post Office Box @ $20/month × 6	120.00		120.00
SPECIAL EVENTS			
Volunteer Snacks etc.	200.00	100.00	100.00
Victory Party	750.00	500.00	250.00
TOTALS	94,730.00	91,470.00	3,260.00

support: cold cash and in-kind contributions. The more you can get donated in-kind, for things like the headquarters office with built-in telephones and insurance, the more cash will be available for expensive things such as printing. On the other hand, it may be wise to retain control of design and schedule by *not* relying on the donated services of a local graphic artist.

Both the amounts and the details in the sample budget are rough approximations. Don't take them as the true cost of any item.

There are some important things to note about this budget. The first is that 45 percent of the total is spent on the cost of direct mailings to voters—design, printing, mail house production, and postage. There are two reasons for this allocation. One is that printing and mailing are very expensive. But more important, direct mail is widely regarded by campaign professionals as one of the two most effective campaign techniques (the other is face-to-face voter contact by the candidate or a person advocating a measure).

Candidates running for state-wide offices or large, well-funded initiative efforts may spend big chunks of money for TV advertising, but at the local level it is a letter in the mailbox that gets the job done. Campaigns typically spend 45 percent to 50 percent of the budget on direct mail solicitation.

Another thing to note is what's missing: the cost of opinion polling. I've left this out of the budget because it is an expense that is most frequently incurred long before the actual campaign gets underway. The results are used to persuade the governing authority to put the library measure on the ballot. Often, the library or the governing agency can pay for the opinion poll, especially if people's needs and desires for library services are being measured. Of course, a very sophisticated and well-funded campaign could build ongoing opinion polling into the budget.

Another item not budgeted is the cost of an important tactic: phone banking. Telephoning is another standard technique (it will be discussed in chapter 10) that relies on good lists of the targeted voters, a revolving pool of volunteers, and a comfortable place with multiple telephone lines and instruments. Real estate offices and (surprisingly) banks make good telephone-bank sites. There is no way that a volunteer-based, local campaign can buy this kind of facility. It has to be donated, and the cost is really incalculable.

Some of the cost of the smaller items in the budget—for example the campaign buttons and bumper stickers—can be recovered by selling them at literature tables, public meetings, etc. If the buttons cost 50 cents to produce and you sell half of them at a buck each, you're home free. But it is never wise to produce any kind of campaign novelty, from T-shirts to lapel stickers, with the budget expectation that they will "pay for themselves."

I know a certain Friends organization that invested substantial funds in bumper stickers back in 1994. It planned to sell them for $5 each as a way to raise money for that year's campaign.

The 1994 ballot measure lost, but the bumper stickers were brought out again for the winning effort in 1996. They were used as door prizes at training workshops, and the last of them were finally sold to another campaign in mid–1999.

Finally, this budget envisions hiring a local field manager at the not very munificent salary of $600 per week. The reality is that every campaign needs a totally organized, good-with-people person who is willing to work all hours of the day and night and has her or his own car. And that is just the beginning of the person's qualifications.

Sometimes local campaigns are incredibly lucky: the person exists on the spot, had no other plans for the three months before election day, and is willing to drop everything to work on the campaign. For free. Sometimes, an organization with the right person on the staff is willing to lend him or her out for the duration, carrying the person's salary and benefits.

Whatever the case, you need this person. If you expect to win, you must choose someone for his or her skills, not availability or friendship.

Unlike the library's budget, which is often tightly controlled because it is so scanty, and is furthermore closely monitored by finance mavens at city hall, the campaign budget ought to have some flexibility. There should be enough money so that the campaign can respond if—four weeks out from election day—something totally unexpected occurs.

Suppose, for example, an October rainstorm dumps buckets on the county and ruins every single yard sign. It is probably too late to get more made, but it wouldn't be bad to spend $500 on funny radio ads that bemoan the loss of the signs but trumpet that Measure L for the library is still alive, dry, and looking for votes.

Or more expensively, suppose the number of people requesting absentee ballots jumps from the usual 15 percent to 30 percent thereby substantially increasing the number of absentee lit pieces that will need to be printed and mailed. A good budget allows for the unexpected.

I'm not suggesting that the budget document, once made, should then be treated as merely a rough guide to expenditures. Indeed, in the chapter on consultants I pointed out that half the disagreements between clients and consultants could be avoided if all parties had agreed to a firm budget with a clear understanding that those limits would be observed. What's most important is to have the resources so that the committee and the consultant can sit down and agree on changes if circumstances demand them—or, if the resources aren't there, can agree to make do with what's available.

The Campaign Calendar

Creating the campaign calendar is an exercise in counting backward. If election day is Tuesday, November 5, 2002, and today is Monday, June 16, it is now 20 "weeks out" from election day. Virtually everything the campaign does over the next four-and-one-half months is targeted to a single day in the future.

So buy one of those big desktop calendars, circle election day, and start leafing backward, filling in crucial milestones. Later we will translate this information into a table that shows all the different things going on in any campaign week.

Here is a list of some of the things, more or less in sequence, that should definitely be put on the calendar:

- Filing deadline for Organization and Disclosure Statement
- Ballot Arguments and Rebuttal Arguments Due Dates
- Filing deadlines for Contribution and Expenditure Forms
- Consultant Contract Addendum Signed
- Consultant Payments
- First Fund-raising Mailing
- Follow-up Fund-raising Mailing
- Fund-raising Visits Begin
- Fund-raising Target Dates
- Begin Endorsement Solicitation
- Absentee Ballots Mailed
- Absentee Literature Piece Land Date
- Sample Ballots Mailed
- First Literature Piece Land Date
- Yard Signs Installation Date

- Telephone Banking Begins
- Get Out the Vote Plans Complete
- Endorsements Complete
- Newspaper Ad
- Get Out the Vote Activities

Virtually every one of these campaign events has associated subevents that must also be put on the calendar—in fact, it is the scheduling of the subevents, such as when the absentee mailing piece must go to the printer, that makes the calendar such a useful document. So, sticking with the hypothetical campaign outlined in the budget above, let's develop some of the elements of a sample calendar.

Start by filling in the known official dates: election day, dates for reports on contributions and expenditures set by the electionscommissioner, the day the ballot Arguments and the Rebuttals are due, and other information you can gather by querying the Elections office: the date voter registration for this election closes, the date the elections commission will mail the first round of absentee ballots to all who have requested them, and the last date a voter can request an absentee ballot. For your own sanity, also note when payments to the consultant are due.

Next, working with the campaign consultant, agree on the date by which the planned mailing to all absentee voters should go out. If the consultant advises that it should "drop" or "land" (this is campaign lingo, and means the day the mail piece drops or lands in the voter's mailbox) on Tuesday, October 8, write in that date. Then count backward to when the piece should be at the mail house for labeling and sorting, when the graphic artist should have finished the design and layout and handed it off to the printer, and therefore when finished copy should be given to the designer. Write in all these events on the calendar.

Go through the same exercise for the mailing aimed at each branch constituency (the Regional Target piece), the yard signs, and so forth. Remember to allow lots of time at the printer and the mail house because every other issue and candidate on the ballot will be giving these people business too.

How much money and when it will be needed is one of the reasons for doing the calendar exercise. It is all very well to be confident that the campaign can eventually raise something on the order of, say, $91,000. However, if you don't have $7,500 on October 24 to pay the mail house to release the Regional Target mailing piece scheduled to land on Tuesday the twenty-ninth, the whole campaign could be in big trouble.

Or think about the fund-raising operation. If you schedule the mailing party, which is going to stuff, seal, and put labels on the major solicitation letter, for June 19, you are going to need $3,500 to pay for the printing, the envelopes, and the reply cards the week before that. And you'll need another $950 for the postage on June 20.

Some campaign events don't require money, but they do require bodies (i.e., volunteers), and it is very useful to know how many will be needed for which tasks, and when. For exam-

ple, suppose the plan is to use a list of endorsers in the giant display ad that is going to run on the final day before the election. Ad copy must be in by October 28, which means that a list of all endorsers, checked and checked again for spelling errors, needs to be ready by the previous Friday. Getting endorsements, especially from organizations, can be a very tedious task, especially since half the groups on the list of potentials will not be meeting during the summer. So a team of volunteers (maybe four people) must be assigned to take on the endorsement tasks and follow-up work. On the calendar they should be scheduled for August and September.

When you have done as much scheduling on the desk calendar as you can, it is time to translate the notations into a campaign calendar organized by weeks and days out to election day and beyond. The objective is to show everything that's going to be going on at the same time. You could use a good computer scheduling program for this, but here we'll do it the hard way.

Studying the result of this exercise reveals some truths about ballot measure campaigns. One of them is that a lot of the work and activity occurs behind the scenes, getting ready for the big public push near the end. An obvious example of this is fund-raising, which is discussed in the next chapter.

But look at July, August, and early September, when the literature pieces are being designed and printed, the endorsements being collected, and (perhaps) the yard signs put up. This

WEEKS OUT	JUNE	JULY			AUGUST					SEPTEMBER					OCTOBER				
	20	19	18	17	16	15	14	13	12	11	10	9	8	7	6	5	4	3	2
BALLOT LANGUAGE																			
ARGUMENTS PRO				10th															
REBUTTAL					17th	24th													
REG TARGET LIT PIECE																			
Write/Photograph										XXXXXXXXXXXX									
Design/Layout															XXXXXXXXX				
To Printer																			
To Mail House																XXXXXXXXXX			
Land Date																		XXXXXX	
ABSENTEE LIT PIECE																			
Write/Photograph								XXXXXXXXXXXXXX											
Design/Layout										XXXXXXXXX		XXXXXXXXX							
Print																			
Mail House														XXXXXXXXX					
Land Date														7th					
YARD SIGNS																			
Design/Layout									XXXX										
Print										XXXXXXXXX									
Install													XXXX						
Volunteers #													10						
Take Down																			
Volunteers #																			
TELEPHONING																			
List #1																			
List #2																XXXXXXXXX			
List #3																		XXXXXXXXXX	
Volunteers #																10	10	10	10

WEEKS OUT	JUNE	JULY			AUGUST					SEPTEMBER					OCTOBER				
	20	19	18	17	16	15	14	13	12	11	10	9	8	7	6	5	4	3	2
FUND-RAISING																			
Mailing #1	20th																		
Telephone Follow-up		XXXX																	
Major Donor Visits		XXXXX	XXXXX	XXXXX	XX														
Volunteers #	10	20																	
Goals			10%		25%				50%					65%		85%			###
HQ/STAFF																			
Manager On									XXXXX	XXXXX	XXXXX	XXXXX	XXXXX	XXXXX	XXXXX	XXXXX	XXXXX	XXXXX	XXXXX
HQ Open										XXXXX	XXXXX	XXXXX	XXXXX	XXXXX	XXXXX	XXXXX	XXXXX	XXXXX	XXXXX
MEDIA FREEBIES																			
Cable TV Talk Show																XXXX			
Radio KWWW Show				XXXX															
Radio KZZZ Show														XXXX					
ENDORSEMENTS (ORGS)																			
Mail Request			XXXX																
Telephone Follow-up				XXXXX	XXXXX	X													
Board Visits											XXXXX	XXXXX	X						
Ad Copy Final																		XXXX	
Volunteers #			3 on Team																
GOTV																			
Door Hanger Copy																	XXXX		
Print																	XXXXX	XXXXX	
Volunteers #																			

	29th	30th	31st	1st	2nd	3rd	4th	5th	6th	7th	8th	9th				
THE LAST WEEK	7	6	5	4	3	2	1	**ED**	1	2	3	4				
TELEPHONE BANK																
List #1	XXX	XXX	XXX	XXXX		XXXX	XXXX									
List #2		XXX	XXX	XXXX		XXXX	XXXX									
Volunteers #	5	5	10	10		10	10									
						XXXXXXXXX										
						10	10									
SWEET VICTORY																
YARD SIGNS											XXXXXXXXX					

can be a hard time for a campaign. The interesting work that needs doing is specialized—for example, writing the Regional Target literature piece. Volunteers are needed primarily for the boring stuff like asking people for money and stamping envelopes. And the campaign chair's reward for the hard work of these months is to get stopped on the street by a local political honcho (who should know better) and be advised that the campaign had better get going if it expects to win.

The campaign consultant, who will have played the biggest role in scheduling the mailings and other visible activities, is perfectly right in her timing tactics. There is no point at all in sending a major mail piece in September, eight weeks out from election day. It will land in the wastebasket at most voter homes, and even if it is read, it will be forgotten. The same goes for telephoning. And the sooner you put up the yard signs, the more chance you run of losing them to preelection storms or vandalism.

So, looking at the calendar, what can the campaign do to keep volunteers enthusiastic, voters interested, and morale up among campaign committee members and library staff? One thing is to open a campaign headquarters. Have you noticed how many candidates do this every election year? This is an especially nice event if the space is donated and all you have to spend money on is doughnuts, coffee, and a banner. If the campaign is going to be run from someone's living room, you could also have a ceremony to open it officially. That might be even more fun and get special press attention.

The speakers' committee could do an August blitz of every civic organization in town from Rotary to the Soroptimists, giving a campaign pitch. August is a tough month to get speakers, and the program chairs will probably be grateful. The point is to think strategically and tactically about how to be visible without expending any more campaign resources than is absolutely necessary.

The final words on calendars are the same as the ones on budgets: meeting deadlines is important, but so are flexibility and the capacity to respond to emergencies and changing events.

Don't Waste Their Time:
Volunteers and
the Library Campaign

No question about it: volunteers are not only the salt of the earth but are at the heart of the democratic process. Electoral campaigns, whether for candidates or issues, can't be run without them, and thank goodness for that. Otherwise, we'd be entirely the victims of people who use their personal fortunes to buy themselves into office or to pay their pet theories into law. And even these campaigns rely on some volunteer true believers. A look at any campaign plan reveals just how many tasks depend on the work of unpaid people who donate thousands of hours to winning (or defeating) a ballot measure.

A campaign that relies more on volunteers than on money is often called a "grassroots" effort. My dictionary defines the grass roots as the common people who are not ordinarily regarded as politically influential. A current slang moniker for the opposite is Astroturf: "the term describing those nice-sounding grassroots organizations that are really just glorified P.R. fronts."[1]

Although in this book I advocate taking a professional approach to mounting a campaign for a library measure—raising substantial money, hiring polling and political consultants, and following their advice— there is no question that the heart of any such campaign will be the volunteers who not only believe in the public library but are also willing to work for it.

Every campaign action described in this book, from developing a campaign plan to walking door-to-door asking for votes, relies on volunteers. This chapter is about organizing them, recruiting them, using them effectively once you've got them, and, last but not least, dealing with the problems they sometimes create.

Getting Organized

The title of this chapter is taken from the cardinal rule of volunteer management, whether it is an election campaign or a Friends of the Library book sale: Don't waste their time.

There are many ways to waste volunteer time, from failing to have the materials ready when the mailing party convenes to not bothering to train the person in the task she or he is asked to do. If Dede Scott signs up for the campaign in May and doesn't get a call to do any work until September, it is a waste of her time and off-putting besides. We'll come back to other examples of how this rule applies, but here the point is that volunteers should *not* be recruited until the campaign knows what it is going to do with them and when.

If you use the Friends Newsletter to make an appeal ("To win, we'll need lots of help. Check off below what you can do: Canvassing, Telephoning, Office Work, Fund-Raising, Yard Signs, Coffee Parties"), you must be prepared to take the readers up on their responses. You should also know which activities will require volunteers. You don't want to suggest that people volunteer to give coffee parties when the campaign has no intention of using that tactic.

So at the same time that the campaign committee is thinking about strategy, devising the campaign plan and calendar, and recruiting someone to lead the fund-raising effort, it should be looking for an individual to take leadership in managing the volunteers: the volunteer coordinator. The coordinator should be made a member of the campaign leadership committee, if for no other reason than infinite time checking back and forth will be saved if she or he is helping make tactical decisions ("Can you do one more week of phone banking?" "Yes, but the chair had better call Mitch's office and say we still need it—I told them we were done").

The qualifications of a good coordinator aren't much: just someone who is exceedingly well organized, enthusiastic about the cause, detail-oriented, gets on well with people, knows how to say "no" nicely, and has contacts in 500 or so other community organizations. And lo, with the exception of the organizational count, there really are such people!

The coordinator's job includes finding volunteers wherever they are, figuring out which people will be good at which task, reminding them to turn up for their assignments, ensuring that the job they are supposed to do is organized and ready for action, and seeing that they are trained to do it. The coordinator also thanks people, moves volunteers to other assignments if they can't do the job assigned, and in campaigns without paid field staff often ends up being the center of all day-to-day information and work.

One of the coordinator's first tasks is to design a system for tracking the people who come forward. The card file or computer database that represents the volunteer list needs to be organized in such a way that it is easy to access the names and phone numbers of all the people who have said, for instance, that they can do telephoning.

A scan through the latest issue of *Campaigns and Elections* (see bibliography) should give you some ideas for where to look for computer programs to consider. If your campaign decides to stick with a manual file, there are many sample forms available in the literature of campaigning. For example, Catherine M. Golden (in *The Campaign Manager*) offers a neat and simple system.[2]

Golden suggests filling out 3 × 5 index cards with the name, address, phone number, and occupation of each person the campaign contacts. Then use colored stick-on circles to represent each type of work the volunteer can do: blue for phoning, red for canvassing, green for yard signs, and yellow for clerical.

Put the circles along the top edge of the card, folded over so that half shows on each side, and the color is visible from the top. Then the cards can be filed alphabetically in a single shoe box, but it is easy to see all the red cards when you want to pull the people who will canvass.

There should also be room on the card to note every time the person is telephoned and asked for something. That way, the clerical people don't lose track and call someone several times for the same task.

Where Do You Find Volunteers?

The simple answer to this question is "everywhere." Enthusiastic campaign committee members and volunteer coordinators have been known to recruit people while standing in line at the supermarket.

The great advantage a library ballot measure has over most other issues is its informed constituency. Every single person who comes into the library is potentially a campaign volunteer and should be asked for help— not by the staff but via a leaflet or even by a Friend standing in the lobby buttonholing patrons as they leave. How about parents of the preschoolers who come to Story Hour on Thursday morning? They know and use library services and may be willing to give something back to help preserve them.

It is important to remember that people vote Yes, give money, and help out the campaign because someone asks them. If no one asks, very few will bother.

It's doubtful whether a library

can win an election without a reasonably strong Friends or other support organization backing it up. Obviously, this group is the first source of volunteers. They can be recruited through a regular newsletter mailing, a special letter, or people from the Friends or the library board getting on the phone and calling the membership one by one to ask for help.

Campaign Consultant Murray Fishel advises "grassroots" campaigns not to overlook one of their most important resources: kids. He tells the story of a campaign in the Midwest in which his daughter and a friend, both of them on bicycles, distributed thousands of leaflets door-to-door on weekends. Their reward was pizza and presumably the intangible satisfaction of playing an important part in community life.[3] Youngsters can help put up yard signs and distribute door hangers on election day. It is their community too, so use them.

Another obvious source is the members of the library staff and their spouses, significant others, parents, and children. Staff can't volunteer for the campaign during work time, but they are available during the other 16 hours of the day and should be encouraged to form a Library Workers for Measure A (or whatever) organization.

The staff group should be asked to bring their union onboard as well—not only for money (see chapter 8) but also for the bodies that the collective bargaining unit can provide.

Does the library employ high school kids as book shelvers and pages? If so, the coordinator might call up their parents and ask for help.

I've heard from several library directors that their staffs have been reluctant to support the ballot measure effort and therefore were slow to make financial contributions or volunteer their off-work time. Sure, they'll vote for it, but working on the campaign is someone else's job.

The reason usually boils down to staff depression: they've devoted countless hours over the years to making do with very little, and the only reward has been more budget cuts. Now someone wants them to put in extra hours on an election campaign. Well, let the library users do it for a change. It is the citizens' job to raise the money for library service. The library workers are already giving their all.

This is a legitimate gripe. The problem is that if it is allowed to prevail, the campaign may founder. Winning requires everyone's effort, both volunteers and staff. If the staff is not behind the measure, doing whatever they can to support it, volunteers won't be either.

I think the way to persuade the staff that they are needed, and should help if they possibly can, is to confront the gripe directly. State it, declare it to have reasonable origins, and then explain why the staff should rise above their very real feelings and offer their help.

Notice, by the way, that I am using the term *should* here, not *must*. No library director, board, or campaign chair may ever force a staff member to participate in a library ballot measure campaign. It is okay to express one's hope for the best, but it is illegal (not to mention counterproductive) to demand it of people.

Every piece of campaign litera-ture, whether fund-raising letters or the basic campaign brochure, should include a "volunteers needed" message. That means that the volunteer coordi-nator should be looking at every con-tribution envelope that comes in to spot volunteers and transfer their in-formation to the card file.

The same goes for endorsement requests to other organizations. One of the things the endorsing group can contribute is people for volunteer work (its name and money are the other two). An article in the Historical So-ciety's newsletter pitching the measure in local history terms (e.g., with new funds the library can finally get the entire nineteenth-century run of the *Clarion* on microfilm) may produce some volunteers if specific tasks are de-scribed. For example, is the campaign going to put up information tables at

key community gathering places dur-ing October? Ask the Historical Soci-ety membership for volunteers to sit at the one on Main Street near the mu-seum.

Social psychologists tell us that people volunteer for three reasons: to gain power, influence, or access to peo-ple with those qualities ("My friend the governor"); for personal gain ("I'll sell more real estate if I know more people"), and commitment to the issue ("Libraries are important!").

From the campaign trenches, Murray Fishel adds three more: people volunteer for issue campaigns because they know a member of the library board, the director, or other staff. Or they need or want social contacts (lonely older people or youngsters who oper-ate best in groups). Fishel's third rea-son is where we started: people volun-teer *because they are asked*.[4]

Using Volunteers Effectively

Volunteers will return again and again to the cause (often doing far more than they originally intended or anticipated) if they feel that their work is important, well organized, valued, and that they themselves are part of a vital collective effort.

Don't waste their time means that when the volunteers walk in the door for Tuesday evening's telephone bank, the script and the instructions are writ-ten and the calling lists are ready to be handed out. It means building a train-ing component into every task so that

nobody wastes precious time doing it wrong, and every volunteer has the opportunity to feel competent at what she or he is assigned to do.

One important (and sometimes overlooked) way to help volunteers feel their work is important is to spell out *why* the task is being done. It doesn't take long to explain that tonight's tele-phone targets are the absentee voters in the Eastside Branch service area be-cause these people almost always vote, but they have a spotty record of support for tax measures. They are a "swing" group, and the campaign needs them. Or if the task is getting out an important fund-raising letter, the coordinator can talk about the overall campaign budget.

There are lots of ways to help volunteers feel like they are members of a winning team that is working hard for victory. One of the simplest is for the job supervisor to put "inside" information from the campaign into the pretask training effort. This doesn't have to be much, but it does need to be something positive that won't be in the papers: "You know, our campaign consultant says he is really impressed with our first five nights of telephoning. We're getting an 82 percent hit rate, and the definite Yes votes are running 68 percent. That's terrific, and it shows why we have to keep phoning—

so we can get every one of those Yes votes to the polls. You can bet the opposition is working as hard as we are to turn out their No people."

Volunteers also deserve—and respond to—a pat on the back. If the campaign were for a candidate, the advice would be for the candidate herself to turn up periodically at big volunteer operations (canvasser training, the final fund-raising mailing party) to greet and thank the volunteers personally. If the campaign chair and or the library director are well-known and popular local personalities, they should certainly do the same thing. The point, though, is that somebody needs to remember to acknowledge that the people volunteering have lives outside the campaign and should be thanked for helping.

Volunteer Problems

Back in pre–Pearl Harbor 1940 my English mother found herself in Chicago looking for a way to support the war effort at home. She decided to volunteer at the Red Cross and was put in charge of the lunchroom, where the waitresses were a corps of local debutante volunteers. These young ladies had a terrible habit of not turning up for work on the mornings after big parties. Mother got tired of this and finally called them together and told them champagne hangovers were no excuse—she expected them for work on schedule. Alas, Mother soon found herself called on the carpet by her own

supervisor: she had alienated the daughters of some major local donors. Did my mother want to win the war in Europe or not? Then get over it, run the lunchroom without them, or go find a job at Bundles for Britain.

Although in other contexts people sometimes advise coddling volunteers if you want to keep them, in an election campaign there just isn't time for that sort of nonsense. There are a fixed number of days to the election, a finite amount of work to be accomplished, and a strong imperative for everyone to focus on the task at hand. If an individual can't, doesn't, or won't do the job assigned, he or she needs to be placed somewhere else or shown the door. Problems with volunteers boil down to two kinds: unreliability and divisiveness.

One kind of unreliability is failing to come on time or to come at all. It is the volunteer coordinator's task to ensure that people know when they are expected for a job and to call them (or to get the clerical volunteers to call them) with reminders. Catherine Golden says she never telephones somebody and says, "Don't forget to come on Saturday." She thinks that might offend the well-organized volunteer who has written the date down on her calendar.[5] Instead, she calls with some other excuse, such as asking the volunteer to bring a clipboard to canvassing, or saying, "I think I gave you the wrong meeting place. It's at 224 Main Street. Oh you *knew* that? Great! See you Saturday morning at nine."

A harder kind of unreliability to handle is the person who volunteers to do some task and then doesn't do it. For example, suppose Minnie Jones offers to go to the board meeting of an organization and secure its endorsement of the library measure and says she'll write a brief article for the group's newsletter.

Minnie misses the June board meeting because she didn't know the date, and the article doesn't get done in time for the summer issue. In July the Jones family is away on vacation. The board doesn't meet in August. By September the final list of endorsements is being compiled, but Minnie can't make it to the board meeting because … well, you get the picture.

The worst thing about people like Minnie is that they are so nice and good-hearted. They would like to contribute time, but they just can't seem to get things done independently. Aside from writing off that organization's endorsement (or if it is a crucial one, keeping a closer check on the status all through the summer), probably the best thing to do with Minnie is to make sure she spends the last six weeks of the campaign assigned to group activities that are closely supervised.

Alas, people who can't get along with other people—who are divisive—are all too common in the ranks of volunteers. There are the negative people, who object to every suggestion made by someone else or to every decision made by the campaign committee. The Yard Sign committee is going to start installing on October 12? That's too soon, they should wait until the nineteenth. So-and-so should definitely not have been put in charge of endorsements; he never knows what he's doing. Nobody can win an election like this; why are we bothering? And so forth.

If this kind of person insists on hanging around (despite his or her clear conviction that this is a losing cause) most campaign committee stalwarts will get used to ignoring him or her. But the volunteer coordinator should make sure this volunteer is never given any kind of voter contact work to do (stuffing envelopes is the perfect task) and that he or she is kept away from new volunteers as much as possible.

Another divisive type is the "Wouldn't it be better if" person. This person has been there and done that and always has suggestions for improvement. "Do you really think we should go down the blocks in that direction?" this volunteer says to the door-to-door canvassing coordinator. "Wouldn't it be better if we started at the other end and…" Also, wouldn't it be better if the telephone script were reworded, the fund-raising mailing stuffed in a different way, and so forth and so on.

The problem with this kind of divisiveness is that superficially it seems so well meant ("Just a suggestion, dear, I was only thinking of the good of the campaign…") when in fact it is usually an attempt at control. Constant suggestions of this sort distract the job supervisor from the task at hand, who must stop to explain why the telephone script is worded as it is.

I suspect the best tactic with this kind of volunteer is a firm, no-nonsense negative, coupled with refusal to discuss the matter further: "You might be right, Jane, but this is the way I have set it up and this is the way we are going to do it. Will you please get your packet and find your partner? Lynne! Great to see you, thanks so much for coming. I've put you with Marilyn here, and I want you two to…"

One campaign consultant says that suggestions from volunteers are always welcome but only 75 or more days out from election day.[6] After that, campaign discipline is the rule. If a volunteer knows a better way, he or she should write it down and save it for next time.

Pat Sandidge, who coordinated the volunteers in the 1996 Santa Cruz campaign, believes that knowing your people, combined with swift and direct action on problems, is the key to successful volunteer management.

"I would never put a person I didn't know on voter contact work," says Sandidge. "I gave new volunteers office tasks until I had a sense of their skills. And when I had to move somebody who was messing up, I'd try to do it in a nice way, giving them options. But also I'd remember—it's the *campaign* that's important."[7]

A Volunteer Nightmare

Charlie Dane appeared (virtually out of the blue, although it turned out he was a Friends member) at the campaign's first fund-raising organizational meeting. He introduced himself as a freelance communications consultant for computer software companies.

By the end of the meeting Charlie had volunteered to be responsible for raising money from local high-tech firms. He said he had a complete database of software companies in the region that he'd use for a mail solicitation. He would then make follow-up phone calls and visits, and no, he didn't need a partner because he knew most of these people personally.

The chair of the fund-raising committee was delighted and relieved—software companies were an important part of the local economy, and the campaign really needed somebody with access to people inside them. He made sure Charlie's letter met campaign standards, looked over the mailing list, and was pleased to note that each letter was personally addressed to a company president or vice president.

A month or so after the initial mailing the fund-raising chair called Charlie to ask how follow-up was going. No checks had come in from software firms, and he wondered if his volunteer was really at work. "Oh, no problem," said Charlie. "I'm making appointments for visits this week."

Two weeks later, with still no results, the chair was about to call again when he ran into an acquaintance who worked at Software, Inc., a local firm. "Say," said the friend, "I know you're involved with that library campaign. You've got some weirdoes in it, did you know? There's this guy, Charlie Dane? He's been hanging around our office for days, trying to get in to see the president and wanting us to hire him to do public relations work. And he says he's part of the library campaign, which is another reason we should hire him. But I know someone who *did* hire him once, and he's totally incompetent."

There are several actions the fund-raising chair can take. The first should probably be to level with his friend from Software, Inc., although the response needs to be worded carefully or the fund-raising chair might find himself in court defending a defamation charge. He can say the campaign may have been deceived by this guy (he'll check it right away) and then segue into talk about the importance of the library measure, asking for advice and suggestions about how to raise money from the high-tech community.

Next, he should get Charlie on the phone and fire him, telling him the campaign committee will take legal action if it receives any reports that Charlie Dane is using the campaign name or the library to solicit work. He should follow the phone call with a letter, probably signed by the campaign chair.

Obviously, the fund-raising chair should rethink the way his committee is checking out unknown volunteers for positions of importance and responsibility. Charlie Dane was a very welcome "walk on" whose credentials nobody verified because the committee didn't have anyone else from the high-tech community. But since money and business were involved, the chair should have done some asking around. Surely somebody on the campaign committee knows someone in the public relations field who could be persuaded to talk off the record. And the chair should never have let Charlie get away with saying he'd make fund-raising visits on his own. Standard practice is to send teams to visit potential big donors, as discussed in chapter 9.

Finally, the fund-raising chair might devote some creative energy to turning this minor disaster into a win. Suppose the campaign were to write a letter to each of the firms Charlie solicited, apologize for the confusion, explain that the campaign's critical need for volunteers and money had caused the mistake, and go on to pitch the library measure.

8

The Fund-Raising Plan

Like it or not, one of the great immutable truths of campaigns and campaigning is that it takes money to win. Furthermore, the sooner you start raising money, the higher your probability of success. The acronym for this phenomenon is EMILY—early money is like yeast. It grows other money. And there is another appropriate acronym: ELAW—everybody loves a winner, so the more money you raise, the more you will be able to raise.

Fund-raising is very hard work. Most citizen volunteers are not enchanted with the fact that in many ways, the fund-raising operation *is* the campaign right up until the final month before the election. Nor do they like the notion that two of the most valuable things they can give to the campaign are their own dollars and the money they ask their friends to give. Confronted with the need to raise money, all too often they propose events (yard sales, talent shows) that better suit the Parent Teacher Association's campaign to build a new ball field at the local elementary school than they do the time-constrained world of electoral politics.

Given this depressing context, it would be very nice if local library committees could do what the big statewide issue campaigns and candidates do—hire professional consultants whose sole function is to run the money-raising operation. These people are experts at framing solicitation letters, developing and cultivating target lists of potential donors, and managing the complicated business of ensuring that what needs reporting gets reported. If your campaign can afford a pro, hire one, and read on only so you'll know what the pro is doing for you.

But if every penny you raise must go to the campaign itself, this chapter has some information about how to do it. It discusses the fund-raising committee, the fund-raising plan, and the projected size of gifts. Chapter 9 goes on to describe and detail the types of fund-raising activities. And while both chapters pass on some of the very sensible advice and rules from the experts about how to raise money, they also try to translate this information into local library campaign terms.

As in most of life, practice often varies from the ideal. In library elections, where the primary actors are not necessarily experienced campaigners or fund-raisers, the gap between the two can be very wide indeed.

It is also important to note that in past years the majority of campaigns for library operating funds or building projects have been run with remarkably small budgets—indeed, most campaign professionals would call the budgets laughable. Despite that, a surprising number have won.

However, times are changing, getting tougher. Unless there is a real revolution in the way Americans conduct their local decision making at the ballot box, libraries going to the voters for funds will be forced to run campaigns that rely on money as much as they do volunteers.

If the examples in these chapters seem extreme (e.g., $100,000 campaign budgets), remember that the techniques for raising money translate down to very low amounts, as well as up to very high ones.

First and Last—The Legal Requirements

Every state has election laws that specify everything from when the local election clerk must mail out the absentee ballots to the regulations for counting the votes. Most crucially in this body of law are rules for raising money: who may donate how much, how what has been raised and spent must be reported, and when those reports must be filed. Get this information from the election clerk, build the reporting dates into your campaign calendar, and make sure that every campaign fund-raising volunteer understands the rules that apply.

Some fund-raising rules have more to do with ethics and image than with the actual law. For example, I once witnessed a city council campaign in which one of the leading candidates was defeated because she borrowed a mere $500 from an out-of-town developer who may or may not have had an interest in a local project.

Nothing can ruin a winning campaign effort faster than the news, five days out from election day, that the campaign committee has accepted an illegal $5,000 gift. And it can happen if you haven't paid attention to the rules.

Getting Started: How Much Do We Need and When?

Most campaign experts would advise that fund-raising start a year or more ahead of the proposed election date. Realistically, however, this kind of advance work frequently occurs only when the library has lost an election and has decided to go back to the voters at the very next opportunity—a year or eighteen months down the road.

More likely, the campaign leadership will start serious work in January for a November ballot measure and will have the fund-raising committee in place by February. Organizing this group any later than that could seriously hamper the campaign.

Chapters 5 and 6 discussed the three parts of the campaign plan: the strategy, the budget, and the calendar. The latter two documents are the answer to how much is needed and when.

But there is difficulty here that it is important to understand. Much of the real planning for a campaign (and thus the budget making and the fund-raising target) is often done very late in fund-raising terms—in June for a November election, after the campaign consultant has been hired and after the measure has been officially placed on the ballot.

The only way around this bind is to get the fund-raising operation going as soon as possible, setting the dollar target at a best-guess figure for planning purposes, and knowing that you may have to increase it if the plan demands it. The calendar in chapter 6 specifies fund-raising in July and August, with visits to potential major donors all the way to October. This kind of late effort can work if the fund-raising committee is very well organized, hitting the ground running, as they say.

The Fund-Raising Committee

Confronting the need to raise significant dollars, most campaign leadership groups should certainly see the necessity for finding a special person with special skills to head up the fund-raising operation. Indeed, one reason for setting even a best-guess money goal right away is to put some realism into the campaign planning effort.

It is not unknown for an enthu-siastic supporter on the leadership committee to believe that raising the money for the campaign will be a mere matter of holding a big event and sending out a letter to the Friends of the Library mailing list. Crucial time can be wasted in the early days if this theory of fund-raising is allowed to prevail. A way to avoid it, and to get on with the serious business of raising big bucks, is to find a good person to chair the fund-raising committee and a committee to help.

Professional campaign fund-raiser Derek Hackett says that the campaign fund-raising committee doesn't need to represent the voters of the district. Rather, it should represent the district's *moneyed* members. And the chair should be someone who is not only committed to the cause but is willing to make the biggest contribution—the maximum permitted by law. According to Hackett, a good campaign fund-raising chair knows where the money is in the community, has experience asking people for it, has time to spend on fund-raising, and is willing to ask other people for money.[1]

And where does one find someone who meets these criteria? Of course your group may already have onboard just the wealthy, experienced person you need. But if you don't, try asking people in leadership positions in the local political parties—not to serve themselves (although their help is always useful) but to suggest people who might be good candidates.

Remember that support for public libraries crosses party lines. There could be a Republican or a Democratic businessman (and 75 percent of the time it is a man) who is unwilling to spend a lot of time raising money for the party but would be very willing (perhaps even flattered to be asked) to work for an apple pie issue like library funding.

Now here's a dream scenario that might work particularly well in a special election: you manage to recruit both a Republican and a Democrat to serve as co-chairs of the fund-raising committee. They end up (in a very polite way, of course) dueling for the title of best fund-raiser and your campaign money troubles are over. Well, if this doesn't work out, another place to look is the leadership of previous United Way campaigns.

Hackett also says that the best people to have on the committee are *sales* people, "particularly sellers of big ticket items or financial investments, such as stock brokers, insurance agents, real estate brokers, and car dealers."[2] Why? Because these folks are used to asking for money, used to trying to persuade people to part with money, and used to rejection—they don't go home in tears if a customer refuses to buy a life insurance policy. Instead they reformulate the proposal and try again, which is exactly the skill they'll need to raise money for the library campaign.

Now it may be that your Friends organization or other support group does not have a lot of insurance agents or car dealers among its members. Surely, though, there are some financial and tax advisors. And if you can recruit a couple of these people, they may be able to bring in one or two more of their friends and colleagues. And what about your friends from Soroptimists and Rotary? And the person who worked so hard on the capital campaign for the church expansion?

Hackett advises groups to be careful not to mistake fund *givers* for fund-raisers, but if you apply the experience criteria that should be easy to avoid.

Planning Is All

The fund-raising committee's first task is to make a plan for raising the money needed for the campaign. It must develop a list of fund-raising activities (events, mailings and phone solicitation, and face-to-face requests), set dollar goals for each of them, and create and stick to a fund-raising timeline that is based on the campaign's overall needs.

All the fund-raising experts are adamant about the need for a carefully structured written plan that answers basic questions about each fund-raising activity: what is going to be done, why it is being done, who's going to do the work, how much money the activity is going to raise, and crucially, how much time and money it will take to do it. That last question is particularly useful in evaluating proposals for bake sales and cocktail parties.

Furthermore, the fund-raising committee must do this work quickly, because you can't raise money without it. And the quicker the campaign gets money in the bank, the easier it will be to persuade the donors of big gifts that contributing to the campaign effort is worth the money.

It is a matter of psychology and our friends EMILY and ELAW. Your message is that the library campaign is going to win because you know what you are doing—look, you already have $10,000 and you just started last week. You're asking community leaders for money, you have a major mailing to a significant "A List" scheduled for March 1, and you have a team of people talking with... etc., etc.

Size of Gifts

The professionals will also tell you that as much as half (anywhere from 35 percent to 50 percent) of all money raised should come in large gifts. Another 25 percent to 35 percent should be in midrange amounts and the final 25 percent to 30 percent in small amounts. The definition of *large*, *midrange* and *small* depends on the total campaign budget.

This only makes sense. A statewide campaign that spends multimil-lion dollars wouldn't consider a gift of anything less than $5,000 as "big." The average library measure campaign deals with a much smaller reality.

Defining the size of gifts also depends on the fund-raising experience and traditions of your community. In many places the business community is used to coughing up contributions for ballot measure campaigns and candidates and expects to be asked. In others, most campaign money is raised

Table F
Raising $100,000: Projected Gifts

Percent of Total Target	Amount To Be Raised	Individual Gift Amount	Number of Gifts Required	Number of Prospects Required @ 5 X Number
8%	$ 8,000	$2,000.00	4	20
32%	$32,000	$1,000.00	32	160
10%	$10,000	$50–$750	14–20	70–100
20%	$20,000	$250–$500	40–80	200–400
20%	$20,000	$100–$249	80–200	400–1,000
10%	$10,000	$100 or less	250+	1,250

from individuals because corporate management lives out of town or the economic climate is very poor.

Whatever, you need to consult with others who have raised money locally for issue campaigns, consider the wealth or poverty of your constituent groups, talk to the pros who work on the campaigns for elected officials (state senators, congressmen), and make your target decisions based on all these considerations.

Suppose you decide that a large gift is $1,000 or more, and your aim is to raise $100,000. If you plan or expect to raise 40 percent of your money from gifts of $1,000, this means you need 40 of them. Of course the more gifts you have that exceed $1,000, the better and easier it will be for everyone. Midsize gifts would then be $250 to $750 where another $30,000 is needed, translating into as many as 100 gifts. The remaining fund-raising target must come in "small contributions"—gifts ranging from $25 to $249.

Viewing the fund-raising target in these concrete terms is certainly de-

pressing. It is a terrible jolt to confront the reality that more than 30 people (30!) are going to have to be persuaded to give $1,000 to the library campaign. In fact, to most library supporters, a gift of $100 or more is "large" or at the very least "midrange." You yourself may never have given more than 25 bucks to a political cause, and that one did not involve a tax increase. How can the campaign possibly raise this kind of money?

The fifth column in Table F, which summarizes these projections, is even more depressing. It shows the number of prospects who must be contacted to achieve the required number of gifts. This is a standard five-to-one fund-raising formula. It does give clues, however, as to which of the three categories of fund-raising activities are appropriate for which targets. For example, planning to contact over 1,200 people for "small gifts" implies a mailing.

But first let's deal with where and from whom the campaign is going to find that $50,000 in gifts from $500 to $2,000.

Sources of Campaign Funding

The campaign fund-raising committee can immediately cheer itself up if it takes a good look at what its resources really are. First, the chair has contributed $2,000, and three other $1,000 gifts have been pledged by members of the campaign leadership. Second, the Friends of the Library is a 501(C)3 not-for-profit organization. It may contribute up to 30 percent of its budget in any fiscal year for advocacy purposes.

This is a place where strategic planning is crucial. Suppose it is now February. The election is next November. The Friends fiscal year runs from July to June. The Friends (and any other nonprofit in the same situation) can make *two* maximum donations to the campaign: one in the current fiscal year and one next year.

The next step is to make a list of all the organizations and individuals who can be asked for money and to set target amounts for each. The fund-raising committee, which is supposed to comprise people who know other people, should be good at this. Their task is to name the people, corporations, and organizations and to make a guess at how much each might be good for. Later they will figure out who is the best person to make "the ask."

One of the best displays I ever saw of this process occurred during the Santa Cruz 1996 campaign. Fresh from a campaign training institute, I spent a lot of my nonwork time writing a fund-raising plan, figuring out how many gifts in what amounts we'd need,

and so forth. But I couldn't get anyone on the campaign committee to buy into it, or buy into it seriously enough to actually start raising money.

Then the campaign hired a political consultant from out of town who asked that we convene a meeting to talk about fund-raising. This was the first actual 1996 campaign activity, and more than 30 people turned up, some of them under the impression that the subject was merely campaign planning. The consultant gave a very inspiring talk about the need for discipline over the coming months, about how we could win with an all-out effort, and about how the campaign was going to target voters branch by branch with mailings and phone calls.

This led the consultant easily to the subject of money—in fact, the campaign was going to cost at least $90,000, which meant we had to raise $6,000 per week or $857 per day between now (July) and November. How would we raise it? Gifts of $500 or more were going to be crucial. So let's start a list, right here and now, of who might give it to us.

"Come on," said the consultant. "Give me the names of people who you think might give $1,000 to the library campaign." One of the campaign leadership team called out a name, and the gathering rapidly took on the air of a revival meeting:

"How about Sally Spade for $1,000?"

"Naw, $2,000 at least."

"Not since she lost that hotel

development deal.... I think a thousand max."

"Okay," said the consultant, writing rapidly on a flip chart, "We'll put her down for $1,000. Who else? Who owns that factory I saw driving into town?"

A high point of this meeting was surely when the husband of one of our trustees stood up and said, "Usually, my wife and I discuss these things in advance. But I'm going to take a chance here without talking to her. We *were* going to give $1,000 to the campaign, but now we're going to double it!"

My personal lesson here was that often it is the outside expert who has the authority to get people moving in the right direction. Our consultant never said anything about fund-raising that I had not said for months before. But she was taken seriously in a way I never could be because I'm a librarian, not a professional campaign consultant. She could (and did) answer any question with the preliminary phrase, "My experience is that..." The other point is the technique the consultant used: getting people to brainstorm names.

Inevitably, some organizations will come up in this process ("We should try the Teacher's Union—they support libraries, don't they?"). Here's a place where the library staff (after hours, of course) can be particularly helpful to the campaign. There is the union that represents the staff and will certainly have a political action committee prepared to donate funds. There are the vendors who have been doing business with (and making money from) the library for years, and who stand to gain if the ballot measure passes. While staff members should never, ever solicit campaign money from a vendor themselves, they can certainly provide names that are a matter of public record to the campaign committee.

The outcome of this exercise ought to be a longish list of donor prospects. The committee's next job is to figure out how to approach these people or organizations and to go on to plan the other types and timing of activities to raise the rest of the money and have it on hand when it is needed. They are discussed in the next chapter.

Two Fund-Raising Nightmares

The first fund-raising nightmare is by far the most common and fortunately, with a hard-nosed fund-raising chair in charge, can be solved. Every campaign has at least one volunteer—call her Ms. Gadfly—who knows everything, has been there and done that, and refuses to be persuaded of anyone

else's point of view. She listens to the fund-raising plan, nodding appropriately at the news that most important is finding people to make contacts with potential donors for major gifts.

When the meeting leader says that $30,000 will have to be raised in this category, and asks the group to start naming names, Ms. Gadfly pops up and proposes running a progressive dinner at committee members' homes. "If we sold the tickets for $25 each we could raise maybe $1,500. Wouldn't that be great? And it would be a lot of fun, too. We did that for the Symphony, you know, and it was *very* popular."

The Ms. Gadflys of this world can be very destructive to the internal workings of the fund-raising committee, among other reasons because the group must spend time trying to keep her on track and beating back her suggestions. Apart from murder, one thing the chair can do is to give her a "small event" assignment with the stipulation that she must recruit her own committee from outside the existing campaign volunteer pool and that no campaign funds will be available for expenses.

For example, Ms. Gadfly could be asked to organize six coffee klatches in six different neighborhoods. The objective could be spreading news about what an expanded library will mean for the local area, raising some money, recruiting a few more volunteers, and best of all, keeping Ms. Gadfly out of the way.

The second nightmare is the same as the one about giving a party to which no one comes. You have a crucial library issue that must go to the voters.

You've thought through the campaign plan, and you know that to win you are going to have to raise some money—say $5,000—for a mailing and some yard signs. But you can't get anyone to give you any money. Oh sure, one of the board members has offered his real estate office for a Get Out the Vote telephone party, but in-kind is the best anyone will offer. In fact, one woman known to be sitting on a minor fortune loftily told the campaign chair that she thought giving money for an election campaign put the library in the same category as all those vulgar candidates for political office.

What *do* you do? Actually, there isn't much you can do, except to rue the day you ever suggested that the way to solve the library's long-term funding problem was to go to the voters for a tax increase. It is pretty obvious that the community needs a healthy dose of reality, so if you are prepared to be patient and persistent (and isn't that one of the things they *did* teach in library school?), losing a tax election may be all for the best. Then, as you do the debriefing afterwards, you will have the exquisite pleasure of pointing out where actual cash dollars might have made the difference. And you'll have a base for planning the next round. In the political fund-raising game, it is often too late, but rarely too early, to start raising money.

Ask, Ask, and Ask Again

The first rule of fund-raising is the title of this chapter: ask, ask, and ask again. The methods for asking fall into three basic categories: holding fund-raising events, asking people face-to-face for money, and doing mail solicitation. The first can be the least productive, the second is the least pop-ular because it seems to be the hardest, and the third is everyone's favorite— because it is anonymous and relatively painless to the volunteers who do the work. The fund-raising committee's job is to distribute the fund-raising effort among some or all of these ac-tivities and set dollar targets for each.

Let's Have a Bake Sale—No, Let's Not

The trouble with most special events is that they take a lot of time to organize, eating up valuable volunteer effort that might more wisely be spent on direct phone solicitation or visiting voters door-to-door. And all too fre-quently they don't raise enough money to justify the effort. One reason is that most events require volunteers to sell tickets, and people hate doing that. So the event relies for its success on sales at the door—not a very secure invest-ment of time or effort for the cam-paign fund-raising committee.

There are some arguments on the positive side for events, of course. They are a good means for publicizing the campaign, making it clear to the pub-lic at large that there are people work-ing on the library measure. A "low ticket" ($5) reception five weeks out from election day that draws 500 peo-ple to drink coffee, eat cookies, and hear an inspiring speech from the campaign chair can be a major morale boost for the campaign volunteers.

But do the math: 500 people at $5 apiece, less expenses, is probably only $2,200 out of a total campaign need of $100,000. This kind of event may well be worth doing, but not necessarily for fund-raising purposes. And do you really think you can get 500 people to get into their cars on a Sunday afternoon to come downtown to hear a pitch about the library campaign?

On the other hand, here are two special events run by library campaigns in California that illustrate why, under the right circumstances, they can be worth doing.

The Pasadena Public Library was on the ballot in March 1997 for a 10-year extension of an existing special library tax. Like all California tax measures, it required a two-thirds affirmative vote to pass.

The Pasadena Library Foundation raised $49,000 for the campaign via a reception at a large private estate. The owner contributed both the place and the catering. "Patrons" were invited for contributions of $1,000 or more, which raised $27,000. Another $22,000 was raised via tickets sales at $75 each.

The $49,000 raised from this single event was 43 percent of the entire campaign budget. Pasadena had other gifts of $1,000 or more, but the vast majority were generated by the special event, which was aimed at the income level of a large group of library supporters. The library won with 86 percent of the vote.

Up in Northern California, the Solano County Library was on the ballot in June 1998 for a ⅛-cent sales tax. The library staff, blocked by law from campaigning during working hours, organized what turned out to be the ultimate bake sale: a series of food events aimed both at themselves and the public. Baked potato sales, baked goods sales, candy sales, a doughnut sale, a spaghetti feed—the focus on food (plus a Tupperware party and a garage sale) raised $4,300, or 9 percent of the total campaign fund-raising effort. The staff estimates that they put over 300 hours into it, which is $13.33 raised per hour.

Bake sales are time and labor intensive, but it is very important to note the other advantages: the effort gave the staff a way to participate in a process that was crucial to its future, and it told the public buying doughnuts that the staff cared about the ballot measure.

Face-to-Face Requests for Money

Campaign experts often say that the most successful fund-raising technique of all is face-to-face solicitation. The reason is that it is the most personal, giving the people making "the ask" the chance to answer the prospect's standard question, WIFM—what's in it for me.

Most people who make major gifts to issue campaigns such as a library ballot measure do so because they believe in the cause. The "what's in it for them" is their conviction that the community will be a better place, the children better educated, and the town more attractive to businesses if there is a decent public library system.

So the fund-raising committee's task is a bit easier than it would be if it were raising money for a political candidate (who is often forced to gather financial support on the basis of implied promises for personal services). The committee can build its case for the ballot measure on the basis of an ideology already in place. Its task is to shape the message so that the prospect will have a lot of trouble saying no.

The committee's first step is to take the list of people and organizations who are prospects for major gifts and figure out who is the right person to make each approach. The lead person for the approach should be a friend, even if the friend isn't on the committee or isn't the best talker in town. The friend should be partnered with someone from the committee, especially someone who has already made a major gift to the campaign. The idea is for the friend to get the door open and for the committee person to explain why this campaign, for this ballot measure, is the right approach to saving, protecting, or expanding public library services here in Great Forks County.

Despite the assumption of a shared bias in favor of libraries, the pitch should be couched in terms of the interests of the prospect, which is why you have found a friend of his or hers to help. Joe Blow is an executive at the county's biggest insurance agency, and your instinct is to pitch the measure in terms of what's good for the library is good for business. But the friend points out that Joe has been a steady supporter and coach at the youth basketball league. So you talk about libraries as after-school havens for kids who can't do sports and tell the story of the dad who came in last fall to ask for a soccer rule book. What you are doing is endeavoring to put the library and the campaign in Joe's terms at the same time that you appeal to his good citizenship and known convictions about the institutions of the community.

As always, planning is everything. Nobody should approach a potential major donor without thinking through the asking strategy carefully and rehearsing who is going to say what. When the friend calls the prospect for an appointment, he or she should make it clear that the topic of discussion will be the upcoming library campaign. And at the conclusion of the pitch, the visitors should be clear and direct about how much money they are asking for.

Aside from belief in the cause, the main reason people give money is *because somebody asked them*. The primary reason they *don't* give is *because nobody asked them*.

Derek Hackett lists five other reasons why people don't give.[1] One is because the request isn't specific enough. People like to give for concrete purposes, such as 500 yard signs or the cost of a special mailing to the constituents of the Eastside Branch. People also don't give if you ask them for the wrong thing (such as yard signs when only a year ago the prospect wrote a letter to the editor bemoaning the environmental damage caused by the campaign advertising of political candidates).

They don't give, or don't give enough, if they have too many choices. It is therefore important to tailor the ask message to a specific amount for a specific purpose (e.g., real estate developer Sally Spade is asked for $1,000 to buy radio time during the last week of the campaign).

Finally, people don't give because the wrong person asks them. The principle of "asking down" may apply here: the first richest asks the second richest, who asks the third richest, and so on. In the fund-raising business, there is a lot to be said for peer pressure.

There is one more rule from the professional fund-raisers that particularly applies to face-to-face solicitations: always ask for the highest amount you want from a prospect, and always ask for more than you think you can get. You can come down if the prospect says no, but it is very hard to go up from your opening request. Prospects are often flattered to be asked for more than they can afford, and anyway, if it is more than he or she can afford, the prospect will certainly tell you so.

Sending the right people to ask the organizations on the major donor list is pretty easy to figure out: members of the organization are the obvious choice for the lead. The solicitation should directly relate to the group's interests, and organizations too should be asked for specific amounts. Each should also be asked for advertising space in its newsletter, either for money or for a get out the vote message near election day.

The union that represents the library workers is a wonderful fund-raising resource, not only because it can make a major donation itself, but because it should be willing to supply help in approaches to other unions. And the unions can be very smart about raising money. In Solano County the political action committee of the library workers' union (which represented a lot of other government workers as well) made an initial contribution and then offered to match other major gifts. By the end it had contributed $13,000 and had been responsible for upping the ante from several other groups and individuals.

Send Money: Mail and Phone Solicitation

Direct mail solicitation can be expensive (first-class postage, printing costs, etc. add up), but most library campaigns should plan to raise 30 percent or more of the total target via this method. Aside from the solicitation letter and other details, which are discussed below, and remembering to enclose a "remit" card with an endorsement box on it, two things are crucial to success: a good mailing list and telephone follow-up.

Lists, lists, lists. Everybody has them, from the Friends of the Library to the local museum association. So do the political parties, and so does the staff of that state senator who has been in office for decades. The best ones are called "A Lists" because they have been used time and again to raise substantial money for candidates and causes on one side of the political spectrum or another. In some communities owning and maintaining the progressive or conservative A List is as powerful a political position as being chair of the local party committee or holding office.

The library measure fund-raising committee's task is therefore to get the community's best A List if it can and to combine it with a Friends of the Library list and any other lists it can get by whatever means. For example, the symphony's concert program probably lists all this year's donors. How about the genealogical society's annual report? Or the fund-raising list the school bond advocates used last year?

It is important to consolidate these lists, pulling duplicates and verifying names, before they are used. You may be surprised by the outcome of this process: sometimes it can turn out that the A List you moved heaven and earth to acquire has an extremely high redundancy rate with the Friends of the Library membership list. At any rate the more names and addresses you have for a mass fund-raising mailing, the more money you will probably raise.

One other thing must be done to the list before it is used for a mailing: it must be checked against the people

whom the committee hopes will make big donations and *the names of those donor prospects must be pulled.* Why? Because you don't want Sally Spade, whom you expect to give $1,000, to get away with writing a pro forma check for $25 in response to the fund-raising letter. No, Sally is going to get a personal visit from two people who know her, with the hope that she'll come up with the target or even more. And if you don't have time to pull names, be sure that "big gift" donors get visited before the mailing goes out.

Many campaign consultants see mailings as a very poor way to raise money. In their excellent book, *Winning Local and State Elections,*[2] Ann Baudry and Bob Schaeffer point out that a 2 percent return rate is regarded as good by experts, and that isn't much compared to the usual expense. Because the success of the mailing is only as good as the list to which it is sent, they recommend a pre-test if you are mailing to five or more people.

For a pre-test, you choose a sample of the list and mail them the fund-raising letter. You then count the returns to calculate whether the mailing produced a net gain vs. its costs, broke even, or actually lost money.

Baudry and Schaeffer may be right in candidate campaigns, but for library campaigns I don't think they are realistic. On the one hand, I can support their point with personal experience. The 1996 Santa Cruz campaign put out a mailing to 4,000 potential donors organized by zip codes tied to the location of branches. There were five letters, signed by five different sets of community residents, plus a flyer about library needs and the remit envelope. Just think, if you will, about the task of getting five sets of signatures from people all over the county, each of whom may have suggestions for text changes in the letter. Volunteers did the sorting, labeling, and stuffing.

For a mailing that cost over $3,000 and brought in perhaps $9,500, the whole thing seems, in retrospect, awfully complicated but in the end worthwhile and highly functional. The return rate was over 10 percent. It informed 4,000 people that the campaign was in operation and had some major themes, such as that if the sales tax passed every branch would benefit.

The Friends of the Library constituted at least half the list, and as a group they are a better target than most campaigns' potential supporters are. The reason is that they understand library services because they use them. They know what recent budget cuts have been, and they understand what increases in service can do for them. Other issue campaigns, as well as candidates for office, have to make these points from ground zero. Libraries with Friends mailing lists are starting with an informed and committed constituency.

Baudry and Schaeffer also point out that people who donate money have an investment in the success of the campaign and should therefore be invited to help ensure it. In other words, they should be asked, and asked again, for money. For example, the donors of small gifts in July can be targeted with a September mailing that explains that the campaign is about to start radio advertising and needs $2,500 to buy the airtime. Or every donor of $100 or more could get a special thanks in the mail, which includes a request for another generous gift.

The best advice I've ever read about how to raise money by mail comes from Chuck Muth, a Republican political consultant. He wrote a "Political Advisor" column for *Campaigns and Elections* magazine about using direct mail.[3]

Muth tells us to read our junk mail before we toss it in the wastebasket. Look for solicitations that catch your attention, he says, and figure out why they are good. Is it the headline? The graphics? The topic or the content of the message? The name of the person who signed the appeal?

All of these are significant considerations in writing effective mail solicitations for money. And since very few library ballot campaigns can afford to hire the really big-time design consultants who do this kind of thing for a living, it is important to keep our eyes open for good ideas we can copy.

Here are some additional tips, gathered from Muth and other sources:

Make the mailing as personal as possible. Use a typewriter-like font on the envelope, and a "live" stamp (first-class postage if possible, but a real stamp even if it is bulk-rate). Ideally, fund-raising letters should be personally addressed, but this is highly expensive and therefore best suited for follow-up letters to midrange donors.

A cheaper tactic is for volunteers

to cull through the addressed envelopes, pulling names they know, and writing personal notes on the bottom of letters (e.g., "Jane, I hope you and Bob can give—the library is so important! [signed] Sue").

Begin the letter with a catchy headline. Here are the headlines on three solicitations I received in the mail the other day:

- From Caribou, Maine to Malibu, California ... We cover every inch of American politics. (An ad for the *Almanac of American Politics 2000*)
- Did you know there is a way to help young people avoid a path of drugs, crime and violence? Art! The Community Youth Arts Project provides an alternative now for at-risk youth in our region.... (A fund-raising appeal from the local Community Youth Arts Project)
- Here's the amazing story of Annet and her family and their cow named Grace. (A fund-raising appeal from Heifer Project International)

Chuck Muth asserts that the first thing people read when they open a direct mail letter is the top of the first page. Then it's highly probable that they'll scan through to the signature and the postscript.

The top, then, should have an attention-grabbing headline that sparks the interest of the reader. The headline should use action verbs, such as *betray* or *save*, and paint a picture in the mind of the reader, such as that cow named Grace. The Youth Arts Project headline above is much too long (headlines should be limited to 17 words), but the

phrase about avoiding "the path of drugs, crime and violence" gets your attention.

Muth lists words that work well, all of them short. *You* and *free* are two of the best. So how about this headline for a library fund-raising letter?

Here's the truth about your free public library—it's starving to death!

The letter should be as long as it needs to be to tell the story. If your mailing list is 100 percent library Friends who have been receiving a steady stream of library news for the last several years, the letter can be a bit shorter. It can remind people of the library problem (framed in terms of the benefits to the reader), explain why a ballot measure is now necessary, and ask for money to support the campaign.

If the mailing list is broader, the letter needs to provide more detail. "The more you tell, the more you sell," says Muth.[4] Use everyday language, short sentences and paragraphs, and reader-centered phrases (e.g., "your kids," "your business," "your home").

Ask for specific amounts of money, and always start with the highest amount. Conclude the letter with an appeal for funds, listing a range of gifts: the highest amount you hope for, a middle amount, a low figure, and an "other" category. And make the need urgent: "Won't you send us a check today? We are fighting to save our public libraries."

Find the biggest name you can to sign the letter. The "biggest" is the person who is the best known in the community, be that an elected official, a prominent businessperson, or the former Olympic gold medalist who is now a local coach. Name recognition helps sell the library message. And be sure the signature is printed in blue. Not black, not red, not green, nor any other color. Blue, because it contrasts with the type and looks more authentic.

Use a postscript to summarize your request. Muth's experience is that people read the P.S. before they read the main body of the letter. So use it to make a succinct and urgent appeal: "Your help is needed today to save our public libraries!"

Include a return envelope and return postage if you can. Every one of us who has ever solicited memberships or raised money for anything knows that the response rate increases substantially (Muth says up to 33 percent) if a return envelope is included in the mailing.

A more difficult issue is whether to pay the postage on that envelope. Will donors be more likely to mail a check if the campaign has provided them with a stamp? Or are library supporters the kind of people who write checks, have stamps on hand, and don't care about the added postage? If the postage paid envelope bears a message such as "Your stamp saves the library campaign money," won't some of the cost be avoided?

A good way to handle this conundrum is to figure out the cost/benefit ratio. Suppose your mailing is to 4,000

people, and you want to raise a minimum of $13,000. Your printing and other costs will total $3,000. Based on local experience, you think you might get a 10 percent return rate, or responses from 400 people, whose gifts would have to average $32.50 each to make the target. Paying the postage for those 400 gifts would cost $132 plus $100 for the prepaid postal permit.

Now suppose you were able to generate another 50 gifts simply because the mailing included a stamped return envelope. Fifty gifts at $32.50 each is $1,625. That's a "profit" of $1,393. I'd say the benefit exceeded the cost of including postage.

Always say thank you and then ask for more. The conventional wisdom (and surely what our mothers taught us) is that everyone who gives money should get a thank you note in the mail. The problem is that this kind of good manners costs $0.33 times the number of gifts. But when you do the math, it may not be as expensive as you think.

Four hundred responses to gifts will cost $132 in postage, and that response has some other very real benefits. It strengthens the friendship of the recipient because so few people bother to say thanks these days, and the donor will therefore be grateful and impressed. It also provides the campaign with a chance to tell the donor more about campaign plans and to ask for more money, this time for a specific project such as a newspaper ad or yard signs.

A less expensive strategy is to get

telephone volunteers and anyone else who can be recruited to take lists of donors home and call them to say thanks on behalf of the campaign. The volunteer says the same thing as the letter: thanks, and here's how you can help some more.

Never forget the first rule of fundraising: *ask, ask, and ask again.*

10
Campaign Tactics: One-on-One Voter Contact

Setting up a table in front of each branch library, staffing it with volunteers from the Friends organization, and training them to answer questions about the upcoming ballot measure is a standard and very simple campaign tactic. So is deploying volunteers to stand on street corners holding up big VOTE YES FOR LIBRARIES signs during the last days before the election. Bumper stickers, buttons, straw hats with special bands are all para-phernalia that campaigns can use to get their message to voters.

This chapter and the next one are about six major tactics that require more effort and planning than simple tabling or button sales. This chapter discusses one-on-one contacts with voters—phone banking and door-to-door canvassing—and the next discusses campaign Web sites, yard signs, absentee voter contact, and GOTV (Get Out the Vote) activities.

Phone Banks

Telephoning voters—to raise money, to find out how the campaign is doing, to get out the vote on election day—is one of the most productive tactics a campaign can use. It may be second only to door-to-door visits to voters as a method for getting votes.

Well-funded campaigns state-wide

or in big districts for candidates or issues expect to spend substantial amounts of money on telephoning. They typically hire professional phone bank firms with automated equipment—outfits that can use 10 workers to make up to 30,000 telephone voter contacts in remarkably short periods of time.

But down at the local library campaign level, we are probably talking about volunteer phone banks, used to identify Yes voters and advocate for the measure. For this sort of do-it-yourself phone banking, there are a number of key points to consider in planning for success.

Collective phoning is better than at-home phoning. In some circumstances (for example, thanking donors for gifts and asking them for more), it is certainly okay to ask trained volunteers to take lists home to make calls. But for Yes-voter identification or advocacy phone calling, working from target lists, it is vastly preferable to have a central place for the telephoning.

The volunteers get more done when they are working under the eye of a supervisor and in a situation where others are doing the same task. The group setting also promotes camaraderie and team spirit, which in turn produces a higher phone contact rate. It is also much easier to maintain quality control of both the message and the data keeping in a supervised setting.

Find a good place. What is needed is a comfortable, pleasant office environment, with five or more phone instruments and lines—the kind of place that is open to the public from 9 A.M. to 5 P.M., but is closed in the evening. The space must be donated, of course. Law offices, insurance firms, a local labor hall, travel agencies, and real estate offices are the most likely sites, but don't hesitate to look for the unexpected.

In the 1996 Santa Cruz campaign we used the brand new offices of a local credit union to which many library staff and county teachers belonged. It had modular workstation cubicles that were perfect for quiet (but collective) phoning. Since the credit union's computer people were there until midnight, the money was locked up at closing time, and the custodial staff didn't come in until 10 P.M., we had the run of a perfect place with no security problems.

Make a written agreement with the space donor. Clearly state what hours and dates the campaign will use the office, who is in charge, and who is responsible for the keys and locking up when you leave. The phone bank supervisor should remind volunteers that they are using other people's space (the desks), so "clean and neat" should be their watchwords. And the supervisor should police the area at the end of every phone bank shift to be sure that all traces of the campaign have been removed.

(Then again, certain "traces" might be desirable. On the last night of Santa Cruz phoning our campaign coordinator, Pat Sandidge, left a Friends of the Library coffee mug on the desk of every credit union worker, and a big "THANKS!" banner over the staff entrance door.)

The telephone script should be written out; work with the campaign consultant to develop it. The content of the script depends on the objective of the telephone bank—to raise money, to persuade undecideds to vote yes, or to get out the vote. Read deButts reminds us that telephoning "is a personal affair." The phone call may be the only contact the voter has with the campaign, so the script should be brief, conversational, and honest.[1]

Here's one of the phone scripts the Santa Cruz campaign used when contacting absentee voters living in the Scotts Valley Branch service area:

Hello, is ___ home? My name is ___, and I'm a volunteer calling to talk to you about Measure B for Libraries, on our local ballot this November. If passed, Measure B will allow the Scotts Valley Branch to extend hours and improve services for children. Do you know about Measure B? [*No one will know about it.*]
    If Passed, Measure B will help:

- Allow the Scotts Valley Library to open on Monday and additional evening and weekday morning hours;
- Increase services to children, including adding a homework center to assist children in learning;
- Double the size of our facility to serve more people and house more books.

Every dime raised by Measure B is dedicated to local libraries in our community. Measure B is supported by parents, teachers, civic leaders, and library users.
    Can we also count on your support for Measure B?
    [*Instructions for tallying responses*]
    Great! With such a long ballot, we're concerned that voters will forget to vote on local issues. Would you be willing to put a small "YES ON B" sign on your lawn or window to remind your neighbors to vote?
    [*More instructions about how to respond to questions*]
    Thanks very much for talking with me. Good night.

In print this script seems denser and longer than it was as a spoken conversation with a respondent. Ninety seconds is a good target length, although again, it depends on the objective.

Notice several things about the Santa Cruz script (which was written by the campaign consultant). First the caller identifies him-or herself by name, hoping to establish a personal relationship. Even in laid-back Santa Cruz we asked our volunteers to use their full names, not just "Sue" or "Ken."

Second, the script says at least twice what the measure will do, based on the campaign themes: increase open hours and expand services to children. And since this message was targeted to Scotts Valley voters, what the measure would do for the Scotts Valley library branch was noted. It also hit another of the campaign themes: every dime will go for libraries.

Finally, the name of the ballot measure—Measure B—is used no fewer than six times. The question about the yard sign added a backdoor seventh use.

To summarize: the script should talk about what the measure will do in simple, uncomplicated language, and it should use the measure's title several times to promote name recognition.

Recruit telephone volunteers wherever you can find them, trying for people who have pleasant voices and can follow directions. One strategy in a multibranch system is to ask supporters from each library facility to take a turn staffing the phone bank for an evening (e.g., "Wednesday is the Scotts Valley Branch night") regardless of which voters are the target. Sometimes service groups who support the measure can be persuaded to volunteer.

Santa Cruz discovered that phone banking was an ideal job for off-duty library workers and especially their spouses: they were used to intelligently comprehending and following directions, they had backup information at their fingertips, and they had an obvious personal investment in the whole enterprise. And staff commitment was impressive to the other volunteers.

Santa Cruz also discovered that, with certain exceptions, men were far more effective than women with one of the target lists—the Republican men over fifty. These voters were less likely to hang up on a male voice, and they really listened when our volunteers told them the Republican candidate for State Senate had endorsed the measure.

Our prize exception to this gender bonding was an experienced psychiatric nurse who had the sweetest voice and most compelling delivery imaginable. She could talk the birds out of the trees, and did—shift after shift after shift.

My point is to think carefully about matching the volunteers to specific calling schedules. *Don't* put the girls from the local college's service sorority on the phones the night you are planning to target a difficult swing-vote group.

Provide backup materials such as FAQ sheets and campaign brochures to the volunteers. One night of telephoning will give the committee a list of frequently asked questions if it doesn't already have one: how much money will be raised? how long will the measure last? who will oversee the spending? will the branch in my neighborhood benefit?

Answers to harder questions ("What about that big retirement raise the county workers got? That money could have been spent on the library!") should be written out on the Frequently Asked Questions (FAQ) sheet. Also, volunteers who don't feel comfortable debating, or simply don't know the answer, should be instructed to tell the person someone from the campaign committee will call back.

Develop a tally sheet with instructions for how to use it. Targeted phone lists (e.g., absentee voters in Dusty Plain) can be set up so that they list the name, address, phone number, district and precinct of the voter, and have three options: Support, Oppose, and Undecided. The telephone volunteer circles the response, with clear instructions to circle "Support" only if the person firmly states they do. Any doubt at all means "Undecided" and hang up means "Oppose."

At the end of a shift, the volunteers go through their lists and fill out a tally sheet that shows (besides the name of the volunteer and the date) the number of voters reached and the totals for support, opposed, and undecided. Hash marks with four lines and a diagonal fifth are *not* desirable because they are too easily misread. Give the volunteers a sheet to fill out. The tally sheet is then used by the supervisor to prepare a report for the shift.

Start each shift with a training session. One important way campaigns build enthusiasm and commitment among their volunteers is by being organized in the job to be done and clear about expectations. Every phone bank shift should start with a brief training session (5 to 10 minutes) in which the supervisor updates the volunteers on the campaign, providing some "insider" information that enables them to feel they are in the know and part of an important effort.

The supervisor then rehearses the objective of the shift's phoning, goes over the script if it is a new one, gives the other standard instructions, explains the rules for tallying results, and hands out a packet to each volunteer. The packet contains a single-sheet set of written instructions, the FAQ sheet, campaign brochure, and a calling list.

Conveying the need for accurate reporting is important. With the best of intentions, enthusiastic volunteers can misrepresent the strength of the measure's support unless they are admonished to circle "Support" only with a definite Yes from the voter.

The shift supervisor's job. The shift supervisor should convey knowledge and enthusiasm, get all the volunteers started on time, and keep them working until the end of the shift (quitting 15 minutes early is five phone calls per volunteer not made). New volunteers need to be mentored and assured that phoning will get easier as the shift wears on.

The supervisor should continually circulate, answering questions, bringing people cold drinks or more calling lists, and listening to what the callers are saying. Spotting the chatty woman who is ignoring instructions to keep the phone calls brief gives the supervisor a chance to correct the behavior sooner rather than later. And if it can't be corrected, the volunteer can be reassigned.

What time do you call? What time do you get telemarketing calls at home? 6 P.M. to 9 P.M., right? My own conviction is that nobody should be bothered by a phone call, even for an important library electoral issue, after 8 P.M. That opinion may be based on all the years I've spent as a working parent longing to sit down at the end of the day and *not be bothered by anybody*.

But I also think that two hours is about the right shift length for volunteers.[2] They get going, they hit their peak, and then it's over and they get to go home and have dinner—enthused enough to come back another day.

Door-to-Door Canvassing

Persuading someone to vote yes on an issue (or for a candidate) is a lot like raising money for a campaign: you have to ask. In fact, you have to ask, ask, and ask again. One way to do that is to couple your mailing effort with going door-to-door, talking to people about the measure, giving them campaign literature, and keeping track of where they stand. Canvassing (or "precinct walking") is normally used to persuade likely voters to turn out and vote yes and to convert swing voters to the cause.

This campaign tactic is not suitable everywhere: rural areas where there are large distances between houses don't make for very good door-to-door efforts. But if your campaign has done an analysis of voter precincts, can figure out where it would be most effective to deploy volunteers to walk and talk the measure, and has a lot of volunteers available, canvassing can be a very good tool.

A canvassing program takes careful advance planning and preparation. The most effective canvassing is done in the last weeks before the election, but the work should start at least two months out. The canvassing coordinator (and for a major effort such as this one there *should* be one person in charge) starts by going to the elections commission and securing precinct maps of the entire electoral district, or those parts which are going to be canvassed. The maps are photocopied and then cut up into individual precincts and blown up large enough so that the street names and addresses can be easily read.

The canvassing coordinator also secures a voter list of each precinct with names and addresses. If these are organized alphabetically the lists will have to be retyped or reformatted on a computer into address order. Again, the lists are copied and divided so that they can be tied to the precinct maps.

Based on earlier campaign research (see chapter 4) the coordinator works with the campaign committee or the consultant to decide which precincts have the highest priority for canvassing. Unless you like to see your volunteers have doors slammed in their faces, time shouldn't be wasted on precincts with a large number of putative No voters.

Suppose the typical precinct has 500 registered voters, and the coordinator thinks enough canvassing volunteers can be recruited to field three teams of two people each per precinct. Team members cover opposite sides of the street but keep track of one another. So the coordinator once again divides up the map and lists, using a highlighter to outline each map with the designated streets that Team 1, Team 2, and Team 3 will canvass. Then the coordinator looks at the campaign calendar and decides which precincts will be targeted on which weekends. Weeknights are an option, but not a very good one in the fall, when it gets dark early.

How many volunteers are needed? The answer to this question is crucial to the calendar and setting the canvassing target, and it is merely a matter of doing the math. A weekend has three potential shifts: Saturday morning, Saturday afternoon, and Sunday afternoon (you don't win votes by knocking on doors on Sunday morning). That means that with only six people in the field at any one time, the campaign can canvass three precincts per weekend.

But it is a rare volunteer who can do more than one canvassing shift a weekend, because it is such hard work. So to cover three precincts 18 volunteers are needed. And if the coordinator wants to target six precincts per weekend, that is 36 volunteers.

There are other ways to plan a canvassing campaign. The coordinator could look for some volunteers who are willing to work alone (most prefer partnerships) and assign them to cover special locations within a precinct over a series of weekday evenings or days. For example, apartment complexes or mobile home parks could be sectored off in this way and canvassed by a volunteer who lives there.

Or the campaign could decide that the best way to canvass is with an all-out effort the last weekend before election day (perhaps with special door hangers for the people not at home). Forty volunteers will be recruited, and because this is a last-ditch push, everyone will work at least two shifts and three if they are able.

Write a script and create written instructions for the canvassers. Here's a sample script, based on one written for a candidate in *Winning Local and State Elections*.[3]

1. "Hi. I'm ___ *[use your full name]* ___. I'm a volunteer for the library building campaign, Measure A. It's on the ballot in November. Have you heard about Measure A to build new libraries?"

Positive Response: "That's right, Measure A will provide enough money to build a new branch library here on the East Side and add more space at the downtown library." [Go to Step 2]

Negative Response: "Well, it's a measure to raise money so that we can expand the downtown library and build new branches. In this neighborhood the only branch is that storefront over on Sixth Street. The Main Library was built in 1945 and it is way too small." [Go to Step 2]

Hostile Response: "Thank you, I'm sorry to have bothered you." [Go to the next house on the route.]

2. "Could I ask whether you plan to vote Yes for Measure A for Libraries on November third?"

Yes. "That's great! Will you need any assistance getting to the polls to vote? Would you like a bumper sticker, or a button? Would you be willing to put up a yard sign?" [Mark the voter as a 1 on your list, and if she/he needs anything or will take a yard sign, note that on your cards.]

Maybe. "Can I answer any questions about Measure A for Libraries? Can I give you a brochure about what the measure will do for public libraries in our city? Thank you." [Mark the voter as a 2 on the list.]

No or Refuse to Answer. "Thank you. Good afternoon." [Mark the voter as a 3 on your list.]

Plans to Vote No. "Thank you for taking the time to talk with me. Goodbye." [Mark the voter as a 3 on your list.]

It is important to give volunteers easily understood coding instructions: 1 for a Yes, 2 for Maybe, and 3 for No, as well as other symbols, such as NR for "No Response," meaning no one home.

The instructions (which can be printed on the same sheet as the script) should advise volunteers not to argue and to keep the conversation brief and friendly. Volunteers should answer simple questions (how much is the new tax? how long will it last?) but arrange for the canvassing coordinator to telephone the voter if more detailed information is wanted.

The instructions should also include any other procedures ("If no one is home, write NR for No Response next to the name, and put a campaign brochure under the door"). Remind volunteers that it is illegal to put anything except U.S. mail in an outdoor mailbox.

Create a canvassing kit for each volunteer. Catherine Golden, the three-time mayor of Ashland, Oregon, suggests that map packets be created for each canvasser.[4] The precinct map, with its assigned territory outlined, is taped to one side of a manila envelope. On the other side is a sheet of paper large enough for the volunteer to write notes ("Sue Smith will take a yard sign, 232 Austin" or "Joe Brown at 45 Texas Street needs ride to polls"). Inside the envelope is the script with its instructions, the voter name and ad-

dress list, and campaign brochures or whatever handout is appropriate. Each team of two volunteers gets two identically prepared envelopes.

Train the volunteers at the beginning of every shift. On the day of their canvassing shift, volunteers should meet at campaign headquarters or wherever to pick up their map packets, be assigned a partner and an area, get trained, and make a last use of the bathroom.

The canvassing coordinator would be wise to make partnership and assignment decisions in advance because it is important to match volunteers with the neighborhoods to which they are assigned. Positive response will be much higher if the oldest volunteers canvass the area where a lot of senior citizens live, and people always like to talk to their neighbors more than they do to outsiders.

The coordinator should bring the volunteers up to date on the campaign (providing whatever insider tidbits will help make everyone feel special), go over the instructions giving special attention to the coding system, and rehearse the script. The volunteers should then role-play the script themselves so that they have some practice.

They should also spend a few minutes discussing worst-case scenarios and what to do about them. For example, what do you do if the person answering the door has been drinking and invites you in for a beer? (Politely laugh off the invitation and move on quickly.) How do you handle the growling, barking dog? (Skip that house.) The crying baby? And so forth.

Support the canvassers with a supervisor who has a car, a first-aid kit, a list of who is in the field and what sections they have been assigned, and the experience to deal with any crisis. The canvassers should report back to this person when they have completed their assignments, turning in their map packets with annotated lists. The supervisor turns all the packets in to the coordinator, who tallies up the results and is ready to tell the next shift how well this morning's canvassing went.

11

More Campaign Tactics

Creating a Campaign Web Site

Today, campaign Web sites selling the virtues of candidates or ballot measures and offering opportunities to work for and interact with campaigns had become standard tools.[1] A Web site is a highly useful and increasingly popular way to give information to voters, among other reasons because active voters are the most likely to be computer literate and users of the Internet. A Web site also reaches a whole new pool of potential voters and supporters who may never before have paid attention to local or national politics but who can be seduced into action by the technology.

Several of the Web sites used in campaigns between 1997 and 1999 were links from the sponsoring library's home page and look as though they were created by library staff. Frankly, that makes me very nervous. If I were the opposition I would certainly argue that the taxpayer–supported public library has no business creating Web site information about its own tax measure without providing equal time and service to the other side. And I certainly wouldn't want to have to give the opposition yet another forum for its message.

I therefore believe campaign Web sites should be totally independent of the library. They can, however, provide links to important information on the library's home page.

Probably the campaign committee's key action in setting up a Vote Yes for Libraries Web site is to find a competent volunteer to take charge of creating and maintaining it. It is nice to contemplate asking the local high school kids taking a home page design class to help out the campaign. But this kind of site depends on the timeliness of its information, whether it is the campaign's latest press release or a response to a crisis. So the volunteer in

103

charge must not only be dedicated to the cause but available at a moment's notice.

Creating a Web site isn't necessarily expensive. A local Internet Access Provider may well be willing to donate the site. But even if you do have to pay, the cost is very low. Only when you get into acquiring software for interactive communication with volunteers does the price begin to go up.

Aside from the usual admonition that the Web site home page should be attractive, feature the campaign logo, and have a brief summary of what the ballot measure is about, here are some ideas for information and links that could be included:

• The official ballot language, along with the Argument in Favor, or a link to the city or county election department's Web site that has the same information. The latter will also have polling place information, vote-by-mail application forms, and other useful things, so it is important for the campaign to provide a link to this site.

• A detailed explanation of the ballot measure, with illustrative photographs, charts, and graphics. It should include links to the library's own Web site information about its current organization and funding. Even the densest text is readable if it leads with a good headline.

For example, the Web page for the Monroe County (Michigan) Library System's 1997 millage campaign started with "We're Not UPS, But We Deliver 90,000 Times a Year."[2] Now who wouldn't read on with a lead-in like that? The site then delivered two solid pages of information about how the funds would be used and what would happen if it didn't pass.

• A colorful service area map on which the user can click to find out what the measure means for her neighborhood—a new building, more open hours, a homework center, whatever. But whenever graphics are used on a Web site, be sure to include sufficient alternative text, so that the visually handicapped and people using non-graphical browsers are ensured access.

• A question-and-answer section, with more photographs, charts, and graphics.

• Links to special information on the library's own or other Web sites. For example, if the ballot measure is going to pay for more children's services, a link to the library page about services to youngsters and their parents would be appropriate.

• Detailed responses to the opposition's Argument Against and other campaign statements. Chapter 13 discusses when responses to opposition statements are wise and when one shouldn't bother. But the campaign Web site is a good place to take the time to set out why the other side is wrong and the measure's advocates are right. Don't forget the photographs, charts, and graphics.

• Campaign news releases.

Another way that campaigns are using technology is to set up "interactive" features on their Web sites. In 1999 the Steve Forbes for President campaign offered Internet users the opportunity to "Lead an e-Precinct," i.e., to become volunteer recruiters and fund-raisers on the Web. Participants used packaged messages provided by the campaign to send to their friends, family, and others, inviting them into the Forbes campaign. They were rewarded with "a direct Internet pipeline to the national campaign management team over which you can share intelligence, personal observations, opinions and reactions as the campaign unfolds."[3]

This kind of technology falls into two categories. The Web site can offer a simple form for the new volunteer to fill out on-line. Somebody in the campaign office then reads it and converts it manually to the Vote Yes database. Better (but more expensive) is software that sends the information filled out by the volunteer to a database that formats it automatically.

Two other points about the campaign Web site. If your electorate has a substantial voting population that speaks a language other than English, make the Web site information available in that language too. And finally, be sure that every piece of campaign literature and the letterhead includes the Web site URL.

Yard Signs

The best yard signs I have ever seen were used by a firefighter union sponsoring a ballot measure that required binding arbitration of their contract disputes. The signs were yellow and red, which I acknowledge sounds pretty awful, but were very effective at reminding the viewer of fires and firefighting. The top half was yellow, with YES ON C in red letters. The bottom was red, with the message "SUPPORT OUR FIREFIGHTERS" in yellow.

The signs began appearing four weeks before election day, "popping up like flowers" all over town, as a local reporter with poetic aspirations put it. Actually, I am told "popping up" had nothing to do with it. The firefighters spent a full month in advance plotting the location of each sign for maximum visibility. They also canvassed and talked with every single voter household in the city. And they won handily.

Most yard signs aren't as pretty as the firefighters'. They run toward colors like fluorescent pink and black, and the most you can say is that they're hard to miss as you drive down Route 7, which is of course the whole point.

At least one campaign consultant (Murray Fishel, president of Grassroots Political Campaigns) thinks yard signs aren't worth the money most campaigns spend on them. They're expensive, they get rained on, marauding kids knock them down at night, and anyway, who makes a voting decision based on a simple message like "Vote Yes for Libraries!"

I suspect that geographic circumstances and local tradition are the prime determining factors in the decision whether or not to use them. San Diego County in California is 3,777 square miles. It would take maybe 4,000 yard signs to make even the beginning of a visual impact on that large an area. At five bucks apiece, 2,000 yard signs is a lot of money and a lot of volunteer time for putting up and taking down.

In smaller counties and towns, or areas with single highway commute routes, yard signs are more useful. As for local tradition, there are places (Santa Cruz County is one and the whole state of Vermont is another) where if you don't have yard signs you don't have a campaign.

Aside from the obvious advice to use a clear message, a symbol which is identified with the library (yep, an open book), and bright colors (musty brown for the out-of-date collection is *not* appropriate), think strategically about siting. People will volunteer to put up signs or to allow signs to be put up on their property.

After you tell them how far the sign should be pounded into the ground to ensure stability (or how to prepare the ground with a cold chisel to keep the sticks from splintering), you might remind your volunteers to face the signs toward oncoming traffic, not toward the street. I know of a campaign in which a very enthusiastic teenage Friend (and kids with driver's licenses are terrific volunteers for this kind of work) put up 25 signs one weekend. Not one of them was oriented toward traffic, and another volunteer had to be sent out to fix them. It wasn't his fault; nobody told him how to site the signs.

One good place to install signs is on the landscaped margins and dividers of shopping center parking lots, for which you will need the management's permission. Best of all is recruiting the owner of several such centers in your county and getting permission for multiple installations.

Shopping center parking lot signs require maintenance; there isn't a homeowner to take responsibility. So a volunteer needs to be assigned to keep an eye on the signs, resurrecting them when they are knocked down by careless parking or bad weather or vandalized by skateboarding teens or (heaven forbid) thugs in the pay of the opposition.

The date for installing signs is an issue. If they go up in mid–September, when there isn't much other campaign activity (except fundraising, of course) they make the point that the campaign is open for business and on track to victory. But by November 3 they will look mighty shopworn and tacky and may have been up so long as to be invisible. Most campaigns end up going for installation three to four weeks out.

Absentee Voters

Absentee voters come in two categories: Permanent and Applied (as they are called in California). Permanent Absentees are people who always vote by mail—because they are elderly, or disabled, or for whatever reason local law permits. Applied Absentees are voters who request a mail ballot for this election only. The elections commission sets a window of time when they can do that, which usually ends a week or so out from election day.

It used to be a standard campaign tactic for volunteers to go to the elections office every day and pick up the daily list of Applied Absentees. Then the committee would hand-address and mail the literature piece aimed at absentees that had previously been mailed to the entire Permanent Absentee list.

Alas, however, this tactic is getting harder and harder to use because the number of people applying for absentee ballots is rising so dramatically. There is no way that campaign volunteers can hand-address and stamp 3,000 or more requests a week, which is the number the Santa Cruz elections office handled in October 1996. Add to this the latest wrinkle—that some states now allow state-wide voting by mail—and we have a situation in which the old tactics are rapidly becoming outdated.

We do live in the computer age, however, and not surprisingly, the technology is coming to the rescue. Whereas volunteers once made daily visits to the elections office, now somebody from the campaign can go in once a week or whenever and ask for a disk with the list of voters who have applied for absentee ballots between any dates the campaign wants. The disk is used to generate mailing labels, and off the piece goes to the voters.

Absentees are an important target for at least three reasons. First of all, they are highly likely to vote, and they may do it with more attention to the sample ballot (with its Arguments in Favor and Against) than people who go to the polling place. Second, they are an identifiable group, limited in size, to which a special appeal can be sent. The ideal is to time the literature piece for absentees to drop the same day as their absentee ballots.

Finally, in close elections the absentees can decide the outcome. So remember the mantra of all elections: people vote yes because you ask them to. So ask.

Getting Out the Vote

Actually, every tactic you've used in the campaign is designed to do two things: persuade voters to vote yes, and get them to go to polls or to file their absentee ballots. GOTV (Get Out the Vote) is campaign lingo for the activities that occur in the last few days before a Tuesday election and on election day itself. GOTV efforts are most effective in low-turnout elections or ones in which there is a lot of voter apathy.

The important thing to remember about them is that they are not efforts to turn out the people who you *think* will vote yes for your measure. GOTV is about turning out who you *know* will vote yes.

Several of the GOTV tactics have been described in other contexts. The campaign can mount a special last-weekend or election day telephoning effort to remind its Yes voters to go to the polls. Door-to-door canvassing is also an option. So is offering rides to potential Yes voters and mailing reminder postcards.

All of these depend on effective previous voter-ID work (the records kept of the phone calls or the door-to-door canvass). They also depend on precinct analysis in the campaign planning stage, to identify key Yes and swing precincts.

Another tactic is election day poll watching. The poll watcher is armed with a list of Yes voters in the precinct. His or her job is then to track who on the list has voted by periodically checking with the election workers.

At around 1 P.M. telephoners start calling the Yes voters who haven't yet turned up at the polls—conveying a sense of urgency, reminding them that every vote counts, and pushing them to get to the polls. Do they need a ride? Do they need a babysitter? Another big

telephone push comes between 5 P.M. and 7 P.M., trying to get Yes voters to the polls before they settle down to dinner and before the polls close.

Deploying poll watchers at every precinct takes a lot of volunteers, but there are two tactics for easing that problem. One is to concentrate on the precincts with the highest known Yes vote count and the greatest overall importance to the district (see chapter 5). The other is to combine forces with another campaign—say, that of a candidate who supports your measure and is therefore likely to share your Yes voters.

In some communities campaign workers get rid of their excess election day energy by getting out of bed early and papering registered voter households with door hangers, reminding them to vote. This is another tactic that begs for alliances with other campaigns. One reason is that door hangers are expensive to produce, so if several candidates and measures get together to print a slate, the financial burden isn't so great. Another is the tremendous volunteer effort required to get them on the doors before the polls open.

A word of caution, however, on GOTV door hangers and alliances with other campaigns. The joint effort should be carefully negotiated in advance so that everyone is clear about expectations and responsibilities.

If you don't think your volunteer force has enough teenagers or whoever to produce a good number of people for election day morning, perhaps your campaign could buy in with a bigger share of the printing bill. The candidates will almost always appear at the top of the slate (they are at the top of the ballot, after all), but there is no reason why your measure should be in smaller type. Make sure that is stated in the agreement.

I've done GOTV work on election morning twice. In both efforts all the volunteers met at the coordinating office, got our door hangers and lists, and set off into the predawn darkness, ordered to report back for coffee and doughnuts when we were done.

The first time was by far my best experience. I was volunteering for a national presidential candidate who didn't have a prayer of winning, so I didn't have any dreams about the outcome. Also, I had managed to corral my teenage son and one of his friends for the effort, probably by mentioning the doughnuts and forgetting about the legwork. I got to sit in the warmth of the car while they ran up and down porch stairs distributing the hangers.

The second time was in 1994, when we had a library measure on the ballot. We had made a deal with a local citizens organization, and our measure was on the hanger (at the bottom, as I recall, in too-small letters) along with the candidates the group was supporting. My husband and I trudged through the mist, block after block after block, startling people in bathrobes picking up their morning papers and getting lost in the depths of a garden apartment complex that seemed to have no clear numbering system nor exit.

The experience started that election day with cold and depression, and it didn't get much better as the day wore on. At 9:30 A.M., when the polls had been open two and a half hours, in our precinct we were only the fifteenth and sixteenth people to vote. By 8 P.M. television was reporting the wretchedly low turnout state-wide, and by 9 P.M. the library victory party had turned into a wake.

12

The Campaign and the Media

In the election campaign world there are two types of helpful media: the kind you buy with campaign dollars and the kind you get for free. The latter is also called "earned" media.

A journalist I know says I'm wrong about this and that the statement insults his whole profession. There are *three* kinds of media, he says: paid, free, and *news*. I see his point, but the reality is that in electoral politics, news stories are either crises to be dealt with or free advertising for the candidate or issue.

It doesn't take a genius to figure out that the latter type is preferable, especially since local issue campaigns have such a hard time generating any kind of news at all. They therefore spend what money they can on media advertising and work hard to get as much free media attention (and as many news stories) as possible.

This chapter will discuss the paid media first and then the free and news media.

Paid Media

Among the four media formats available—newspapers, television, Web sites, and radio—the first is the most commonly used by issue campaigns, the second is usually too expensive to be a realistic option, the third is pretty

specialized, and the fourth frequently forgotten or has its power underrated.

All require the same basic assessment before a decision is made to use them. To start planning, don't think about the cost of the ads or the Web

110

site. The question is, who is reading the paper or watching or logging on or listening to the station?

Chapter 5 described building a campaign plan around targeting particular segments of the voting populace. If one target is Democratic men and women aged 25 to 50, it would be very dumb to spend any money for ads on the region's leading conservative radio station. Far better to put the dollars into ads during "drive time" on the station that does news and easy listening.

The information about who is listening to a radio station (or watching a TV channel) is set out in the station's "demographics"—the statistical information about its audience the station uses to sell ads. It isn't just politicians and issue campaigns that want to know who's in the audience. Before they will buy time, so does the local garden center, the liquor store, or a car dealership.

Newspapers are required to periodically report their circulation figures (how many paid subscribers, how many other sales, etc.), and that's the information you get from the advertising department. It is up to you, the advertising buyer, to make a judgment about who those subscribers might be.

Let's look at the newspaper, television, and radio venues separately. Web sites were discussed in chapter 10.

NEWSPAPERS

A newspaper with the biggest circulation isn't necessarily the best advertising venue in a local election cam-

paign. These days many communities, especially the ones in large metropolitan areas, are served by both a big-city daily (the *Chicago Sun Times*, the *Philadelphia Inquirer*) and smaller weekly, ethnic, or campus papers that focus on local news, arts, and sports coverage.

These papers are often free (they are supported entirely by their advertising), and they may be widely read locally. Or there may also be a regional daily owned by a national company (e.g., News Media Corporation, which owns papers in the Midwest) trying to do national and state-wide news, as well as local stories.

So in planning how to spend its advertising dollars, the campaign committee needs to make a judgment based on local conditions and election targets. Is it sensible to buy very expensive space in the big metropolitan daily just because it has a large local subscriber base? Your ad will reach your voters but also a lot of unconcerned people in other communities, too.

It might be smarter to concentrate on the local daily, if there is one, and the weeklies. This is not to say that the big-city paper should be ignored. Its editorial judgments and news coverage are probably very important to many potential voters in your community. But ensuring support and good coverage comes under the heading "free media" (and news), not paid.

Newspapers sell advertising by the column inch. The information is set out in a rate card obtainable from the advertising sales department. The newspaper also offers design and layout services, or you can give them camera-ready copy. A common campaign practice is to save the newspaper advertising dollars for the last week before the election and then do at least one big display ad: VOTE YES FOR MEASURE C NEXT TUESDAY!

In 1996 the Santa Cruz campaign took a whole page ad in the Sunday-before-the election edition of our local daily, the *Santa Cruz Sentinel*. It listed hundreds of Measure B endorsers by name, with a copy of a supportive editorial from the larger competitor, the *San Jose Mercury News*, in the middle of the layout. The *Sentinel* endorsed Measure B on its editorial page the same day, so the effect was a double whammy.

As our campaign coordinator explained later to an annoyed *Sentinel* managing editor, the local paper had to expect to pay a price for withholding its endorsement until the very last minute. The campaign would have been glad to use the *Sentinel* editorial in its display ad if it had appeared on time.

The Santa Cruz Measure B opposition also used newspaper advertisements but of a very different sort. With less money to spend, they ran 1 × 3½" ads every other day in the local daily for the last two weeks of the campaign. Targeting their potential No voters, the ads were placed in or near the financial pages of the paper. Most of them were headlined "PROPOSITION B IS A FRAUD." In fact, it was a "Measure," not a "Proposition," but then the opposition was never great on accuracy. The text was about how there would be enough money in the county budget for libraries if

county employees weren't given such generous benefit packages.

My reading of the *Sentinel* rate card leads me to think they spent $84.50 per ad, for a total of roughly $700. It costs a lot less to oppose a measure than it does to win one.

One tactic a cash-strapped campaign can employ is to ask endorsing organizations to sponsor (meaning pay for) newspaper ads about the measure. This is often an attractive option to potential sponsors because it gives the group a way to publicize its own name at the top of the ad while supporting the library measure. The campaign offers enough help to ensure that the ad gets placed at the right time and doesn't contain any wrong information.

This tactic can be used with elected officials too. If your measure is a county-wide one, but you have constituent cities and towns, published support from the local council members can be very important. Persuading them to get together and sponsor an ad in the local paper the last week before the election can provide a real boost for the campaign, not to mention the politicians themselves.

"LIBRARIES MATTER" was the headline of a 2 × 4 display ad in the twice-monthly *Mid County Post*, which came out the last week of October 1996. Five Capitola City Council members and one council candidate, with their names listed in big letters, urged people to vote yes on Measure B, "Saving Our Libraries by Working Together." I am sure that ad had a much bigger impact on prospective voters than regular news coverage of the Capitola City Council endorsement.

TELEVISION

I am going to give television very short shrift for two reasons: it takes real professionals (who cost more money than most library campaigns have) to produce good TV ads, and it is very hard to effectively target voters in a television audience. If you doubt the first claim, just take a look at the dreadful advertising done by used-car dealers on your local cable channel. These ads may draw people down to look at the SUVs and pickup trucks, but I am sure they wouldn't persuade anyone to vote yes on a library measure.

Back in 1972 Robert Redford made a very interesting film about campaigns called *The Candidate.*[1] It presents what is probably the definitive movie word on how media professionals package an office-seeker, or by implication, a ballot measure. The bottom line: only the biggest library campaigns in the largest cities can afford to use television, and their campaign consultants will buy the expertise required.

The other good reason to not bother with the video media is the television market. Even local stations, picking up programming and ads from the networks but concentrating on regional news, usually cover a far broader area than the typical library election district. But their advertising prices are based on their whole market, so the library campaign pays for ads reaching people far beyond its service area. As the cable television industry consolidates, this is increasingly true.

Television news and local programming can be used effectively in an election campaign—but those are media for which the campaign doesn't pay. They are discussed later in this chapter.

RADIO

For a medium that was going to be killed by television, a lot of people sure do listen. National radio interview shows make the print news all the time with what their guests said or did. Local stations are on the air and heard everywhere from the beauty parlor to the car repair shop. People listen as they drive to work, as they do their daily run or walk, or as they sit in the staff lounge eating lunch.

Lots of these people may well be your campaign's target Yes and swing voters, so giving serious consideration to radio advertising is a good idea. For one thing it doesn't cost much; for less than $1,000 a campaign can produce and buy time for quite a few radio spots. For another thing, radio audiences are pretty carefully defined, as the demographics of the station will tell you. There is easy listening, hard rock, all talk, all news, and so forth. Every format has its audience, and the advertising sales people at the station know who those people are.

The cost of a radio ad depends on when it is broadcast. The most expensive time is typically during the morning commute (called "morning drive time")—7 A.M. to 9 A.M. Late afternoon/evening commute time is less expensive and late-night hours the cheapest of all. A station's rate card will quote the cost of different length spots (10, 30, or 60 seconds) at different times.

Judge Lawrence Grey's book *How to Win a Local Election* has a very useful chapter on radio and television. Grey points out that although radio time is cheap, you have to buy a lot of it because the average listener needs to hear an ad 25 times for the message to sink in.

Based on his own campaigning experience Grey recommends 30 spots in the same time slot and spreading them out over several weeks: one spot per day three weeks out from election day, two spots a day two weeks out, and three times a day during the final week, all during morning drive time.[2] He also advises that you buy the time early, before the opposition gets there and takes the time you want.

A 30-second radio spot is roughly 80 or 90 words. It must include a standard disclaimer ("Paid for by the Save our Libraries Committee"), so that doesn't give you a lot of room. The best radio ads are like any other campaign advertising: they speak to the campaign themes (kids, open hours, whatever) in a clear and understandable way, they use the name of the measure at least twice, and they have a good, memorable slogan or catch phrase.

If the campaign consultant has recommended using radio advertising, he or she will write the ad copy. If a volunteer from the campaign committee is writing it, Grey recommends producing at least three versions and snipping and pasting until you get what you want.

Many radio stations offer production facilities to advertisers (they will say this on the rate card, as well as the fee) and can also provide one of their on-air people to do the voice work. Campaigns may prefer to use someone who sounds less slick than your average radio personality.

Try the drama department of the local college to find a budding actor or actress to read the copy if you don't like the way the campaign chair or another volunteer sounds. And if you must do your own production recording, look in the yellow pages of the phone book to find a recording studio.

One final point about radio advertising: it is relatively flexible. In a pinch it doesn't take long to produce a 30-second radio spot. So if you have bought and paid for time during the last week of the campaign, and the opposition hits with an egregious new attack, you can quickly make a new tape responding and insert it in the times you already have scheduled. Or you can run it alternately with your standard ad.

Responding to the opposition has some dangers, however. See the Nightmare at the end of this chapter for an example.

Free Media, News Media

Any library that thinks it has the support to win a tax increase at the ballot box doubtless had an effective public relations program in place long before the start of the campaign. Press releases and public service announcements (PSAs) are probably produced on a regular basis. The task becomes shifting these standard activities into terms that will serve the campaign.

Although the campaign committee cannot sponsor PSAs, the library can certainly step up its efforts to draw attention to its services via this form of free radio advertising.

NEWSPAPERS AND EDITORIAL BOARDS

A ballot measure campaign wants two things from its local newspapers— fair news coverage and an editorial endorsement. Like beauty, the definition of fair coverage is in the eyes of the beholder.

The campaign would like to see every one of its news releases printed (preferably on the right side of page 1 above the fold), and it wants any reporter covering an issue to lead the article with the campaign's point of view, quote the campaign or library board chair extensively, and of course give very small attention to the opposition. Good newspapers, on the other hand, strive for balanced reporting (the Yes people say this, but the No people say that) and tend to mistrust news releases as mere campaign folderol.

One way to close the gap between these two positions is to request a meeting with the paper's editorial board to talk about library problems and discuss the upcoming campaign. This meeting should occur very early in the process—say, when the elected body is agreeing to put a measure on the ballot.

A metropolitan daily paper's editorial board is usually composed of the editorial page editor and the other people who are assigned to write editorial matter for the paper: the editorials themselves and the in-house columns if there are any. Smaller local papers, whether dailies or weeklies, are often put together by tiny staffs (often including the owner or publisher) who have responsibility for everything from reporting the news to writing the editorials. This is an advantage for the campaign because at the meeting the library people are getting to the reporters as well as the editors.

The library board chair, the library director, and the campaign chair should attend the meeting. They should make a brief presentation outlining the library's situation and needs and the justification for the ballot measure. Then there should be a frank and fair exchange of views.

The library people may well be shocked to learn how little the newspaper people know about the actual workings of the library or its funding. That's one of the reasons for the meeting—to inform them and to get across the idea that library supporters and the staff are real people with solid competencies, who intend to run a serious campaign.

The other is of course to persuade the editor, owner, or publisher to support the upcoming library measure. Unless the editors are rabid antigovernment people who see all spending except for police, fire, and streets as "waste," they have every reason to do that because they depend on a literate and informed community. The campaign people shouldn't hesitate to remind the newspaper people of their shared values—the rights of both a free press and free public libraries under the First Amendment.

Statements made at an editorial board meeting are not quotable without permission. Therefore it is okay to give the newspaper people a sketchy outline of the upcoming campaign—not so much to inform them of the details as to make the point that the library supporters have a plan and intend to win.

One request the campaign can make is for the paper to run an occasional op-ed piece about the library, written by (or at least signed by) a well-known local library supporter. These are the 700–900 word opinion columns that run on the page opposite the editorials. They are a wonderful vehicle for conveying information about library issues. Timed right—say mid–September for a November election—they are a free means for contacting voters at a slow point in the campaign.

The editorial staffs of the local papers may well feel that having given time to listen to the library supporters they ought to do the same for the opposition. There's nothing you can

do about that, except to try to extract a "fairness" agreement from the paper.

Urge the editor or publisher to telephone with questions if the opposition raises points that the paper doesn't understand. And if the paper runs an op-ed column from the opposition, be ready with a counterpiece from the library campaign to run as quickly as possible.

In summary, the point about meeting with the editors and other staff of the local newspapers is to create a base of informed understanding. The result will be that when the paper gets yet another news release from the campaign, the managing editor will at least have a basis for making a "run or ignore" decision.

NEWS RELEASES AND NEWS EVENTS

The trick to getting a news release run in the paper, or on the radio or TV, is to put one out only when the campaign has actual news to report. The problem, of course, is that the campaign's version of news is not necessarily the same as the media's. The local TV station does not care that the Sunnyside Neighbors have endorsed Measure D. Nevertheless, the campaign would be wise to produce a steady stream of news releases on the off chance that the story will hit on a slow news day and get run.

Releases should be one page, double-spaced, and written in readable language. They should also include a contact person with a phone number and be addressed to the specific reporter covering the government or election beat. A release sent to the local foreign language paper should be translated; it will almost certainly be used if it is.

More difficult for a campaign is to find or produce events the media can cover as *news*. Candidates for office have a much easier time with this. They release position papers, propose legislation, or visit scenes of local disaster.

The issue campaign, especially one for a tax increase, must be a good deal more creative. And whatever the event is, it can't look too much like a stunt meant to draw media coverage, even if it is.

My ideas run toward things like holding story hour in the vacant lot where the new building will go—every week from September through October, and canceling only when it rains. Or maybe a bunch of Measure D supporters could be persuaded to march on the central library to demand doors be opened on Monday.

Perhaps more important than producing news events is being prepared when news events happen. I once heard a communications consultant define *crisis* as an event for which we haven't prepared. An event may require special handling, but if we've thought it out in advance, it will be much easier to handle.

There aren't many library campaigns that run the risk of the local tabloid catching the campaign chair in a compromising position with an underage library page. But difficult or potentially embarrassing questions certainly can come up.

For example, what does the campaign chair say when a reporter calls up and asks for a response to the opposition's statement that the Yes on Measure D Committee is spending thousands of dollars on an out-of-town consultant? Or what about an announcement by the mayor that if the library measure wins she's thinking about taking some of the existing library money and putting it into building a new parking lot?

The rule here is to anticipate, anticipate, anticipate. Think about the worst-sounding questions the campaign could be asked, and then frame good answers to them.

By "good" I mean responses that are truthful, quotable, and if at all possible, framed in the campaign's terms, not the opposition's. "Yep," you can say "he *is* from out of town. We think our library deserves the best, so we've hired the best to help us with the campaign. You know, it takes more to pass a measure than it does to defeat one." Or, "She said she'd spend it on a parking lot? That can't be an accurate quote because that's illegal under the ballot measure. Besides, Mayor Jones knows how desperate the library is for money. We've got to restore open hours…"

One final point about the news media: appoint a campaign spokesperson, and don't let anybody else talk to the press. The only way to ensure a single message from the Vote Yes campaign is to make sure only one person is talking.

INTERVIEW SHOWS ON TELEVISION AND RADIO

One important kind of free media coverage a campaign can use is the interview shows broadcast on local radio stations or cable television channels. Both require careful preparation but can be very useful for getting the library measure message out.

Radio shows almost always involve call-ins from listeners. This means that the person who appears for the campaign not only needs to know his or her stuff regarding the ballot measure but must be prepared to answer off-the-wall questions about library services in general and anything else a caller thinks up. Therefore it may be a good idea to take two people to the interview show: somebody from the campaign and the library director, who can be knowledgeable about services but neutral on the ballot measure.

Two other points about radio show interviews: First, take along (or even send in advance) a list of questions you would like to be asked. The radio show host may be lazy and not prepared or may simply not have thought of the most interesting questions.

Second, don't bother to appear on the local right-wing radio station, thinking you can convert No voters. All you are doing is giving yourself a hideous half hour or more of flak from the opposition and giving them free airtime to kick you and the library measure around.

Television interview shows tend to be more structured, but they present other problems. The first is that because of the picture on the screen, you are only getting half of the viewer's attention. That means you have to make your points concisely and memorably, using word pictures to convey the information.

Since you are not a famous television personality paid to have a style all your own, you will also have to be careful of twitchy hand gestures, and try to keep a pleasant but serious expression on your face.

Dealing with a hostile interviewer requires special confidence. In fact, it is probably a good idea to rehearse an interview, practicing how to respond to loaded or difficult questions.

Certainly you should watch the show you are going to be on a couple of times to get a sense of how the interviewer(s) handle guests. If he or she is a grandstander (mostly interested in maintaining his personal reputation as the Mike Wallace of Madison County), you should be prepared for that, practicing your confident expression and developing some sound-bite facts to snap back at him.

Ted Koppel of *Nightline* fame offers an interesting perspective on the interview process. "A television audience begins by identifying with the interviewer, not the interviewee," he told Howard Kurtz. "You [the interviewer] have certain questions they wish you would ask. You are their representative. They're with you. How can you lose them? Either by asking totally dumb questions ... or by being too aggressive too early in the interview."[3]

To summarize the rules for handling hostile questions: don't panic and don't get mad. Remember you have the truth on your side, so tell it simply and easily. Keep a pleasant and friendly look on your face, conveying warmth and a spirit of helpfulness, not anger, defensiveness, or complacency. Deflect the question with humor if you think you can, but never laugh at your own jokes.

None of this is easy, but there is a secret about it: even though audiences love to watch somebody ask tough questions, they also believe in fair play, and they root for someone they like. Remember Koppel's point about the audience's being on the side of the interviewer at the *beginning* of the interview: your job is to get them to switch to you, the library, and the ballot measure.

LETTERS TO THE EDITOR

In a lot of places the letters to the editor are the most heavily read section of the local newspaper. What's more, they tend to be read regularly by the people who are likely to vote in any election. As a result, campaigns for and against ballot measures, not to mention the people supporting a political candidate, try to use them to get their messages across. And letters to the editor have another advantage: they are a free way to contact a great many voters.

The local newspaper has published rules about length, signatures, and so forth. It may limit the number of letters it will print on the same subject from any one person, and often may stop printing election letters a certain number of days before the election. It may, too, devote a whole page to election-related letters on, say, each Saturday in the month before the election. This practice is too bad, really, because it means the library measure letters can get lost in the multitude.

The Yes on the Library Measure campaign might think about dividing its letters to the editor effort into two parts. One part consists of the standard advocacy letters, and the other part is letters responding to misstatements from the other side.

Producing the former is a matter of organization. Volunteers are recruited to write letters and then scheduled for the dates they should get their letters in the mail. Telephone follow-up makes sure they do.

If the local daily has a one-letter-per-writer rule, schedule the same volunteers for letters to the weeklies as well (but send different letters to each venue). Try for three or four letters per week, timed to arrive at the paper on different days. Writing letters for the newspapers is an excellent job for people who can't get out much.

A good letter to the editor is concise. It doesn't attempt to cover every campaign theme. Rather, it focuses on one point: "We need our own library branch here in Eastside" or "We owe it to our kids to provide good public library services." It is personal, and it finds a way to use the name of the ballot measure at least twice.

It can be helpful to write sample letters for volunteers so that they have a format to follow, although the results can sometimes be stilted. Another technique is for the best campaign wordsmith to write letters for volunteer signatures. But do be sure to give the volunteer a copy when she or he signs it, so that if the newspaper calls to verify the letter source (some papers do that), the volunteer isn't caught without information.

The opposition is probably mounting its own letter-writing campaign, and this can be infuriating to the supporters of the library measure. The vote no letters will doubtless contain not only hyperbole but actual misstatements. Given the number of people reading the letters to the editor, this can be dangerous.

An action the campaign can take is to find a good writer who will volunteer to take responsibility for producing responses to the opposition's letters. A group of volunteers willing to sign such letters should also be organized.

When a bad letter appears in the paper, the writer volunteer composes a response, takes it to the signer for a signature, and delivers it to the newspaper—all within 36 hours. With the right kind of attitude from the paper's managing editor, the "Truth Patrol" letter should be printed in a day or two.

Letters responding to the opposition may cut into the number of advocacy letters that are run by the newspaper—and that may depress the volunteers who have written them and would like the satisfaction of seeing them appear in print. Therefore it is important to warn volunteers that not every letter will be published and that "Truth Patrol" letters need to have the highest priority.

Both advocacy and response letters can be very useful in drawing attention to the issues involved in a campaign. There's a fairly famous story about a candidate's use of this tactic that illustrates the point.[4]

In this story, the candidate was a newcomer and underdog in a race against a long-term incumbent congressman. The congressman had bounced several hundred checks at the House Bank. Alas for the opposition, however, the news broke many months before the election. The challenger's task was to find a way to get the "scandal" back before the voters in October.

Letters to the editor were used for the purpose. The challenger's campaign recruited people to write letters *defending* the practice of bouncing checks—because it can happen to anyone, because it isn't much of a crime, and because it is hard for a congressman to get by on only $130,000 a year. The effect was to keep the issue in the public eye and to generate indignant letters from people who had nothing to do with the campaign, expressing outrage at the whole business.

As Judge Lawrence Grey points out, the letters to the editor weren't the only reason the challenger won, but they were a very useful means for keeping his issue before the voters.

A Media Nightmare That Really Happened

All through October 1996, the opposition to the Santa Cruz library system's Measure B used the local conservative radio station for daily blasts against the measure. The vehicle was the noon-hour talk show, which usually featured an interview guest and call-ins from listeners. Several of the Save Our Libraries supporters got tired of this and insisted that the campaign buy time on the station for a 30-second ad refuting the opposition message.

The ad was duly written and taped by a well-known local personality. The time was purchased and paid for, and the ad began to run during morning drive time. But on the Thursday before election day, as our campaign coordinator was driving across town listening to the radio station's daily dose of negative call-ins, she suddenly heard an adulterated version of our ad. The vote-no folks, aided and abetted by the station staff, had intercut the Save Our Libraries ad with their own material. In this adulterated ad, each of our spokesman's statements was followed by another voice saying things like, "That's a lie! Plenty of funds for libraries are available. Fight fraud, vote No on B."

Not surprisingly, our coordinator was furious. She switched course and drove to the radio station. She stormed in and went directly to the studio where the station owner was broadcasting. Banging through the door, and completely disregarding his panicked gestures toward the red "ON AIR" light, she verbally lashed him for his unethical behavior and demanded that the tape be handed over to her for destruction.

The station owner countered that the tape was meant as a joke. Our coordinator laughed derisively in his face and made for the control room, where a cowering engineer handed it over.

Various listeners gave our side a clear edge in this encounter, but to this day our coordinator gets angry about it. She says every radio professional she has ever talked with thinks the station behaved unethically. If we hadn't won, she would have advocated taking the station and its owner to court. As it was, we let bygones be bygones, although since then nobody from the Santa Cruz Library staff or Friends organization has ever agreed to appear on one of that station's programs.

There are at least three points to make about this whole incident. The first is that when you give a radio station your taped advertisement master, you are doing it with the understanding (but without the guarantee) that they will treat it ethically. Most stations wouldn't stay on the air long if they treated their commercial customers the way this one treated Save Our Libraries, but then again, all is fair in love and war, and campaigns are definitely war. I suspect that the vote-no people, even though they lost, still think they played a pretty good trick on our side.

The second and third points are intertwined. Why on earth was the Santa Cruz campaign buying ad time on a conservative radio station that was doing nothing but attacking our ballot measure? A small group of campaign stalwarts couldn't stop themselves from listening to the daily diatribes, but none of our base and very few of our swing voters were listening. We wasted money we could have spent for a final week's spots on the station to which our voters did listen. We also provided a classic example of "failure to maintain discipline."

In the last weeks of a hot campaign it is very hard to stick to the plan and ignore the opposition. But it has to be done.

13
The Opposition

Here are some rules about the opposition that any campaign committee should know by heart and post on the office wall:

- It is easier to defeat a tax measure than it is to win one.
- The opposition will hammer at your measure's weakest point—so *what is it?*
- Be prepared to counterattack.
- The opposition often attacks late in the campaign. (This rule is a variant on the one about how "It's not over till it's over.")
- You can't win a debate with the opposition; you can only *not lose.*
- The opposition is smarter than you think and far more capable of dirty tricks than you imagine.

Why is a tax measure easier to defeat than it is to win, even in a state that does not have a super-majority law? Because of the standard rule of thumb that 20 percent of all voters vote no on any tax measure. So right away the opposition has to get far fewer votes than you do.

Furthermore, on a difficult issue such as a new tax, which no one, including you, really *wants* to pay, it is not hard to sow seeds of doubt in the minds of potential supporters. Opposition assertions that twist or ignore facts—e.g., hammering on last year's county staff benefit increases as evidence of available money without mentioning that the employees themselves paid for the increase—can dissuade swing voters from the Yes side.

There are two theories about how to handle the opposition in a ballot measure campaign. One is that the campaign has no choice but to respond because the opposition is telling lies about the tax measure, getting lots of media attention, and eating into the library measure's tenuous hold on a majority.

The other theory is to ignore them, stick to the campaign's message, never respond to their attacks, and believe you can beat them by turning out your base voters plus the swing voters you've recruited to the cause.

Opposition Tactics: A Horrid Example

Before we discuss the merits of either strategy, let's look at a classic case of successful opposition tactics—the San Diego, California, library sales tax campaign that was the sole measure on the ballot in early March 1999.

San Diego County has three million people and is nearly 4,000 square miles in size. The quarter-cent sales tax would have generated $423 million over five years for eight public libraries (with 79 branches) in 18 cities (including San Diego itself) and the county's unincorporated area. All eight jurisdictions endorsed the measure, and serious money (over a million dollars) was raised for the campaign.

In November 1996 a comparable measure got 59 percent of the vote, but California's super-majority law defeated it. Supporters decided on a special election in March because they thought the 1996 defeat was partly due to the library measure's getting lost on a long ballot. The regular election in November 1998 didn't work because bonds for a highly controversial new stadium were on the ballot and nobody wanted to see the library competing with major league baseball.

The consultant (Fred Register) devised a year-long Yes on L/Support Your Local Library campaign that had three phases. March to June was spent collecting organizational endorsements, which totaled 350 by the end of the campaign. From June through October a speaker's bureau comprehensively covered the county.

From November to election day in March the field operation contacted voters with 280,000 phone calls and dropped 1.2 million literature pieces. The targets were what County Librarian Marilyn Crouch called WALRIDs: Women, African Americans, Latinos, Renters, Independents, and Democrats.[1] "We even called Republican women *living* with Democrats," says Marilyn. The campaign also distributed 30,000 Get Out the Vote door hangers to the people they hadn't been able to reach by phone.

By the first week in February (four weeks out from election day) the efforts were clearly paying off. Tracking polls showed the measure with 63 percent support.

Through all of this the opposition seemed to be in hiding. It waited until five minutes before the closing deadline to file its Argument Against the ballot measure. And it made a misstatement of fact in the Argument (that there are no standards for public libraries), which the Yes on L campaign got a court order to strike from the published Arguments For and Against.

Three weeks from election day the mayor of San Diego announced that she was thinking of using tobacco funds (the millions of dollars California cities and counties expect to get from the national tobacco court settlement) for construction of the new downtown library—a project *not* included under the umbrella of the new tax measure but now helplessly associated with it by the mayor's choice of timing. This structure, already a contentious issue, was supposed to be funded by new transient occupancy (hotel room) tax revenues, ostensibly to be generated by the new stadium.

The mayor's injection of this spurious but seemingly related proposal served to infuriate nearly everyone: the health advocates, who had been counting on the tobacco money for anti-smoking education; the people who opposed the new downtown library's proposed location; the Yes on L people, who knew that their ballot measure had nothing to do with the construction project; and most crucially, the antitax people, who had opposed Measure L from the beginning and promptly characterized the mayor's statement as a typical political "bait-and-switch" tactic, one tax for another.

Troops from the Libertarian Party and the religious right joined in an antitax coalition that argued not against libraries and Measure L but against waste in government and taxes in general. Led by Richard Rider, the well-known head of the Libertarian Party, the coalition began hitting every radio talk show every single day, as well as television news and the newspapers. Here's the beginning of a typical letter to the editor of the *San Diego Union-Tribune*: "Prop. L is a con job. The tax-and-spend crowd is trying to bamboozle the citizenry again."[2]

Consultant Fred Register said later that the campaign's hope had been that the San Diego media, especially TV and radio, would downplay or perhaps even ignore the election.[3] But the mayor's trial balloon made that impossible. The San Diego media market is big enough to support local TV stations but not large enough to generate the steady diet of photogenic news stories that its neighbor to the north, Los Angeles, produces. So the electronic media in San Diego is particularly hungry for controversy.

The opposition provided that controversy during the last weeks of the campaign with its accusations of political lying and government mismanagement. While the print media provided editorial support and reasonably balanced coverage, the radio talk shows pounded day after day, and the television news programs gave the opposition equal time.

This put the opposition in control of the information, and the Yes on L people (who knew that their ballot measure had nothing to do with the downtown library construction project) found themselves in the hideous defensive mode of constant response. As Marilyn Crouch commented, "Every encounter during the last two weeks became a debate. And you don't win debates—at best, you don't lose them."

Even if the Yes campaign had refused to talk to the media at all—had "gone dark," as they say—it wouldn't have worked. In order to maintain "balance," the media would designate someone as a Yes person if the campaign didn't produce a spokesperson.

The opposition also ran a dirty tricks operation: phone banking to the Yes on L target voters, telling people their polling place had changed and recommending they call a certain number to get the new address. The number was the Yes on L headquarters, and the effect was to tie up the phones when they were badly needed.

On March 2 Yes on L got just 50 percent of the vote, down nine points from the loss in 1996 and a far cry from predictions as late as three weeks out from election day. The measure passed in only one of 18 of the county's cities and garnered only 23 percent of the absentee vote.

Was there any way this campaign could have salvaged the election once the opposition went to work? Fred Register thinks not. He says that the mayor's highly controversial red herring about the new downtown library, coupled with the peculiarities of the San Diego media market, doomed the measure to defeat. It was the only thing on the county ballot, and the electronic media, with nothing else to cover, had a feeding frenzy.

So let's go back to the rules at the beginning of this chapter. Can we extract any lessons or validation from the San Diego experience, even if the professionals are right in saying this campaign couldn't have won?

Responding to the Opposition

The day after the defeat, County Librarian Marilyn Crouch said she thought the campaign had made the mistake of underestimating the opposition—not its size but its power to seize control of the media. That's a good point, which leads to another one: it is crucial that a campaign, aided and abetted by its consultant, should think carefully in advance about what the attacks from the opposition might be and how they can be countered. Some of this information will come from the Argument Against, which sets out the points the opposition will argue in favor of a No vote.

But the other thing a campaign must do is to envision, if it can, some worst-case scenarios. Nobody in San Diego could possibly have predicted that the mayor, who theoretically supported Measure L, would blindside the campaign with her remarks about the new downtown library. Or could they? If the site and the funding for the new downtown library were such controversial issues, could the campaign have prepared a counterstatement in case it came up?

Or suppose a library has managed to catch the eye of the people who advocate filtering the Internet and those critics suddenly jump into the campaign with a battle cry of "The Library feeds pornography to our children! Vote No on Measure X!" The last two weeks before election day are a very bad time to get trapped in a debate about the First Amendment to the Constitution of the United States. So how does the Yes campaign respond?

In these days of increasing pressure on public libraries to filter Internet access, it would be madness to undertake a tax increase campaign without a policy already in place. And if it has a policy, the library should be able to quickly articulate what it is and the reasons for it.

If what the opposition wants is

filters, the library has to be prepared to explain why it will or will not filter the public access terminals. One thought: "Kids aren't watching pornography at the library because the staff stops them. The problem is at home! That's where they're watching it. Parents need to do a better job keeping track of what their kids are doing and filter their own computers if they want to."

The rule about how the opposition will pound on your measure's weakest points applies here too. Santa Cruz lost a sales tax campaign in 1994 because the ballot measure did not directly guarantee that the county supervisors would spend the money on libraries. It was advisory so that the measure didn't have to be passed by a super-majority.

The opposition, which was tiny but vocal, talked about nothing but the lack of guarantee. They loved libraries, but they were afraid that those untrustworthy elected officials would go back on their fine words and divert the sales tax to something else. The Yes campaign had spent all its preparation time thinking of reasons why it needed the new money and none figuring out how to respond to an antigovernment attack.

Steve Smith, the political director of the California Democratic Party, says that the key to an effective No campaign is to find the one weak spot and fix voters' attention on it. For Yes campaigns, the challenge is to know what that weak spot is and to mount a capable defense.[4]

And remember another of the rules: it's not over till it's over. A well-orchestrated (and well-funded) opposition may hold its fire until virtually the last campaign minute. Producing a barrage of media and literature attacks two or three weeks out from election day doesn't give the Yes campaign much time to respond if it chooses to do so. But the committee will be in a better position if it has gone through the grim exercise of thinking up the most dangerous things the opposition can say and has planned responses.

Ignoring the Opposition

All the examples above support the first of the two theories about how to handle the opposition—respond, because you'll lose the election if you don't. Does that mean that there are no circumstances in which the opposition should just be ignored?

Absolutely not. Judging when and if to respond depends on a collection of factors, including the campaign plan, the size of the opposition, the focus and virulence of their attack, and their timing.

The reality is that if the library tax measure has been carefully written and the local economy is reasonably healthy, the opposition will be composed of the usual suspects: the antitax and antigovernment folks who oppose everything but are usually a minority.

Their argument is with local government and how tax money is spent, not with the library or the need for library services.

These people and their resources should not be underestimated. They can be relentless in their attacks and good (if only because outrageous) at grabbing press attention. Their usual methods often are not worth dignifying with a Vote Yes response.

For example, suppose the opposition has a compulsive letter-to-the-editor writer who begins sneering at the library tax measure back in July and keeps up weekly attacks until election day. This can be very hard to take, especially if half his facts are twisted and the rest just plain wrong.

But the truth is that he is digging himself into a hole. By late September he will have run out of new ways to state his case, and the only people paying any attention to his letters will be his own compatriots. The Vote Yes campaign will waste valuable time if it bothers to respond to his letters and will furthermore call unnecessary attention to them.

Chapter 12 on the media discussed more useful efforts concerning letters to the editor—ones in which the Yes campaign keeps up a steady flow of positive letters and responds quickly to the periodic negatives. That's different from this kind of opposition effort.

Often the Vote Yes campaign will be asked to participate in a public forum or debate about the upcoming election, appearing on the same platform as the Vote No people. These appearances are hard to avoid, so it is important for the campaign spokesperson to take along a group of supporters. Nothing is more depressing than being stuck alone in a room with 40 No voters, even if you know they are the only No votes in the whole county.

The thing about debates is that they are almost always a waste of time. You can't win them because the judges (the audience) aren't neutral—they are already either for or against the measure. All you can do is lose by falling into the trap of trying to correct the opposition's misstatements, which gives them the upper hand in defining what's discussed.

The best tactic in this situation is to stick to the standard campaign pitch and ignore the opposition's statements. If this is impossible, don't argue, but try to turn the opposition points to the library campaign's advantage: "The library can't do anything about how the state legislature is shifting property tax away from counties. But I can tell you how we'd spend new money at the library—by adding Sunday hours and fixing the roof at the Westside Branch."

Sticking to the campaign plan and ignoring the opposition is one of the hardest things library supporters can be asked to do. In the 1996 Santa Cruz campaign, the opposition argued against waste in county government, and the library campaign theme was built around restoring open hours, services to children, and support for local branches. Our principal spokesperson for debate-type campaign appearances was a former mayor of Santa Cruz who was remarkably effective in presenting the library themes. And since he happened to have a lot of experience as an elected official, he was also good at making substantive responses to the opposition's statements.

The Vote Yes campaign supporters loved it, and a group of them decided that the campaign should take a big ad in the local newspapers setting out the response arguments as articulated by the former mayor. Our campaign consultant argued hard that they shouldn't bother, for three reasons:

- Because it is very hard—indeed practically impossible—to respond to an argument without restating it. Why should the Vote Yes campaign give the opposition free publicity?

- Because the audience at a campaign debate or forum is very limited. It may be a big crowd in meeting terms, but count the votes present: 50? 100? What plays well at an event featuring live action (the speakers) does not persuade the other 72,000 voters the campaign needs to get to the polls to vote yes. What persuades them is the carefully thought-out campaign theme and messages reaching them at home. A much better forum for the detailed response would be the campaign's Internet home page.

- Because a display ad for this purpose is expensive and hasn't been budgeted. "But we'll raise special money for it," the supporters said. If they're into raising more money, they should do it to cover the deficit.

It is hard not to be seduced into letting the opposition set the terms of the campaign dialogue but important to remember that *dialogue* is not what a campaign is about. The dialogue occurred back when the elected body agreed to put the tax or bond measure on the ballot. The campaign is about persuasion and getting out the vote.

Campaign professionals who are used to handling candidates for office advise their clients on at least one thing about the opposition that applies to issue campaigns as well. Avoid name calling and personal attacks for as long as possible. That means that when the opposition leader hits the Yes campaign with yet more stuff about how the library wouldn't need money if it charged fees, it may be tempting, but a bad idea, to say something like, "If Sally Smith had graduated from eighth grade she'd know what a dumb idea that is. Don't you love it when rich bitches like Sally tell the rest of us how to live?"

In 1996 the leader of the opposition appeared at my Rotary Club to pitch his Vote No cause. He started his talk by presenting me with a $35 membership check and contribution to the Friends of the Library. I would cheerfully have kicked him but was told afterwards by a friend that I received it graciously.

As it turned out, his gesture did him more harm than good. A couple of days later I ran into a Rotary colleague on the street who said, "You know, his argument isn't with the library, is it? He just hates the county government and is using your library measure for his own cause. Me, I think I'm for the library." You bet.

14
And If You Lose

The Morning After

Some of us probably remember those movies of the forties and fifties in which Hollywood attempted to teach us how to behave in life's worst crises. Bette Davis was often the star—beautifully dressed, valiantly making the best of a bad situation. She knew she had to go down to the library the morning after losing the election, and so do you.

For one thing, you owe it to the staff to turn up before opening time and help everyone work through their angst. I'm not suggesting that you have to arrive whistling a happy tune. But it is your job, if you are the director, to transcend your own dismay, and to put on a stiff-upper-lip performance for the rest of the staff. Sure they'll know its a show—but we loved Bette Davis when she did it, and people will rise to your effort too.

What do you say? What is in your heart, of course. That you feel stung and wounded, just as they do. That you too are angry. That the election results will have to be carefully analyzed to figure out exactly what went wrong. That we don't know yet what losing will mean in terms of service cuts and that until we do the job is to go on meeting the information needs of the citizens of this community. Remember all the people who voted yes; we owe them our best service now more than ever.

You certainly need to agree on a staff line for talk with the public for today and the rest of the week. I'm reminded here of another movie—the moment in *The Right Stuff* when the Russians have been the first to send a man into space and the *Mercury Seven* astronauts are ambushed by the press. John Glenn says (in the script), "Let's face it, we need to be forthright, gracious, and magnanimous and say the Russian guys just beat the pants off us." In the next scene the movie-version Glenn says privately to his colleagues, "I'm TIRED of being forthright, gracious, and magnanimous.... Let's get this show on the road."[1]

What you want to avoid is the staff's making casual threats and comments that could get you into trouble later (e.g., "Well, we're just going to have to close on Mondays, I guess"). Sure, you campaigned on the fact that the library will have to cut hours if it doesn't get more money. But closing on Mondays is a political decision the library board must make, and its members may well have other ideas for how to deal with the catastrophe. More on the board later.

The staff's comments to the public need to acknowledge the problem ("Yes, it *is* too bad—we're very disappointed") without displaying anger, which can all too easily be interpreted as blaming the listener. People may rage all they want at home, but at the library they are forthright, gracious, magnanimous, and sad. No, we don't know what will happen next. Yes, there will certainly have to be some changes, but we aren't certain what they will be. And (because it is good strategy to assume that any library patron interested enough to comment on the election is a supporter) thanks very much for *your* support—we all really appreciate it.

Figure Out Why

The first question the press will ask is probably "How do you feel about losing the election" (which deserves a response like, "Fabulous; actually, it's been years since I had so much fun," but *don't* say that because you'll hate reading it in the paper tomorrow). Remember: forthright, gracious, magnanimous, and sad.

The second question will be, "Does the library plan to go back to the voters in the next election?" And that's the one that requires careful research and thorough analysis of the election data to answer.

Joe Napolitan, a veteran political consultant, says that you can learn more from a losing campaign than a winning one, primarily because few

people bother to analyze the victory.[2] But a defeat should get a close look to figure out why.

It is often pretty obvious. If you got whupped 65 to 35, and there is a group of antilibrary and antitax advocates dancing outside the library even as you open the doors the morning after, it doesn't take a genius to figure out that lying low for a couple of years is the sensible course. Maybe there are some changes you can make that will turn the tide next time.

But if the loss margin was low—say five points, or (even more heartbreaking) only one or two points, going right back in the next election (if state or local law allows it) is a serious option.

To answer the question you need to look very carefully at the election data. Where did you lose? In the precincts you expected, plus down on the southside where the canvassing fell apart and nobody ever got up any yard signs? Was the absentee vote particularly high? Would changing the timing of the last literature drop get the message to more absentees?

Can 80 percent of the reason for the loss be attributed to the other measures on the ballot, which won't be there next time? Is there a constituency (such as people who live in mobile home parks) that didn't vote but could be organized? Is there any reason to believe that the opposition will be tired out by its victory instead of invigorated by it?

The Library Board, Elected Officials, and What's Next

The library board, especially if it includes elected officials, has particularly difficult decisions to make after a losing ballot measure. The instinct of many of the board members (and indeed the library staff) will be to find ways to continue or restore library services even without the money that they told the voters was required. New, often bizarre, funding packages will be proposed or more cuts in behind-the-scenes services suggested. Heaven forbid that the public should suffer. This is especially true if the margin of loss was a big one and there doesn't seem to be any possibility of returning to the voters any time soon.

Since I am not an elected official, I can advocate (just as can any library director) the harder course of action. If you said in the campaign that without new money the library was going to have to cut open hours (because it will have to lay off staff), go ahead and close on Monday. Cut the book budget. Do what you said you would have to do.

Sure, it hurts. Sure, it means some people will lose their jobs, although if you are lucky you can reduce employees by attrition. The point is that libraries and their supporters will never be credible, and will never win voter support, if they keep on finding ways to make do with what they don't have.

Now, this hard-knocks strategy runs counter to the instinct of any elected official interested in staying in office. So the library director and the campaign support groups should do a fair amount of political walking and talking with each member of the jurisdiction's legislative body and the library board before either group has a public discussion of what's next.

One persuasive argument to the elected officials is "trust in government": the people have a low opinion of government that is only confirmed when the legislative body finds a magic bullet funding solution after an election defeat.

When you do close on Monday you will hear right away from the opposition that the library is punishing all the people who voted no. The response to that must be immediate, and it must come from the political leadership, not just the library staff and Friends.

"Punishing the voters?" you say. The library staff is suffering as much from these cuts as any member of the public. We don't have the money to maintain open hours. That's why we asked you to vote for Measure B, and because it was voted down, we're closed on Monday."

Victory from the Jaws of Defeat

After the Santa Cruz City-County Library lost the sales tax election in 1994, library supporters and the board made a careful examination of the arguments the opposition had used and spent the next 18 months fixing what could be fixed. Obviously, there was no responding to the people who oppose all tax measures on principle. But the opposition had also criticized the library governance structure and questioned the library's long-range plans. There had been strong demands that the administration of any new tax should be clearly locked into use for libraries only—not just another money pot the electeds could dip into at will.

The library's needs, however, made it clear that going back to the voters for support would be necessary. So supportive government officials set out to negotiate a new governance agreement among the cities and the county, solving problems that had been festering for decades. The library board sponsored a series of community forums and task forces to get community agreement on the scope of public

library services Santa Cruz County wanted.

The 1996 outcome wasn't much different from the 1994 proposal, but it was repackaged to respond to the articulated concerns of voters—services to children, access to branch libraries, and expanded open hours. And the board of supervisors agreed to place a *designated* sales tax for library services on the ballot, even though in California designated taxes require a two-thirds majority to pass.

Despite the articulated wisdom of several noted local election gurus who said we couldn't possibly get two-thirds, we mounted an aggressive campaign and in November 1996 won with 72.3 percent of the vote.

It hardly needs saying that winning is far better than losing, but it is worth pointing out a couple of things about the results of the 1994 Santa Cruz Library election debacle.

The first is that the library system is governed in a fairer, more democratic way as a result of the post-loss governance agreement. Winning has made it possible to make the new structure work efficiently, which might not be true if we had lost—nothing works as well as money to solve political problems.

The library was also forced to make clear choices about the structure and cost of its services (branches, outreach programs, etc.), which theoretically, at any rate, the public understands. The staff wasn't terribly happy with some of these decisions. For example, the community still wants lots of neighborhood branches, although these take a great deal of money to support. On the other hand, the staff got a few things (like an automation system upgrade) about which the public felt pretty dubious.

The second point about the return to the voters in 1996 was that the vote demonstrated that there is a basic, underlying support for public libraries that we in Santa Cruz County could count on, and probably libraries across the nation can as well. People believe in free public libraries for their kids, for themselves, and for other people.

If you can package a ballot measure that makes sense, and mount a campaign that speaks to community needs and interests, in most situations the people will respond by demonstrating these beliefs by voting yes for libraries.

Learn More About It:
A Note on the Sources

Most of the books and articles written about campaigning are aimed at candidates or the people managing the campaigns of candidates for office. It is necessary to extrapolate and translate these sources into issue-campaign terms.

Books

Asher, Herbert. *Polling and the Public: What Every Citizen Should Know.* 4th ed. Washington, D.C.: Congressional Quarterly, 1998.

Baudry, Ann, and Bob Schaeffer. *Winning Local and State Elections.* New York: Free Press, 1986.

This is a very useful book, but because the most recent edition is 1986, it lacks up-to-date information about using the Internet and the latest research in opinion polling and the like.

Faucheux, Ron, ed. *The Road to Victory 2000: The Complete Guide to Win-* *ning Political Campaigns—Local, State, and Federal.* 2d ed. Dubuque, Iowa: Kendall/Hunt, 1998.

A compilation of the best recent articles from *Campaigns and Elections* magazine. Alas, the editor has failed to cite each article's date of first publication, which is important information when the topic relates to Internet use, e.g., but aside from this librarian's quibble the book is an excellent resource.

Golden, Catherine M. *The Campaign Manager: Running and Winning Local Elections.* Ashland, Oregon: Oak Street Press [886 Oak Street, Ashland, OR 97520], 1996.

Golden has been elected mayor of Ashland three times and has worked on countless local campaigns. This is very much a nitty-gritty how-to-do-it guide for the campaign relying on volunteers.

Grey, Judge Lawrence. *How to Win a Local Election: A Complete Step-by-Step Guide.* New York: M. Evans, 1994.

The judge has run for office quite a few times, and he wrote this book to help other local candidates. He is particularly helpful on details about the media.

Hall, Richard B. *Winning Library Referenda Campaigns: A How-to-Do-It Manual.* New York: Neal-Schuman, 1995.

This is a truly comprehensive work on library campaigns up to 1995, based on Hall's annual articles for *Library Journal.* It features a wonderful collection of campaign literature pieces from around the country.

Schultz, Jim. *The Initiative Cookbook: Recipes and Stories from California's Ballot Wars.* San Francisco: Democracy Center/Advocacy Institute West, 1996.

Despite the silly format and focus on California, this book offers some useful advice on topics ranging from gathering petition signatures to raising money.

Periodicals

Many states have magazines devoted exclusively to the politics of their geographic area. These can offer interesting and informative articles on the local political scene, as well as advertisements for campaign paraphernalia, regional opinion polling consultants, and the like. The national periodical source is:

Campaigns and Elections, the Magazine for People in Politics. Washington, D.C. Congressional Quarterly. Published monthly with double issues in October/November and December/January.

The magazine also has a Web site: *www.campaignline.com.* Every issue is chock-full of useful advice, interesting articles, and of course national political campaign gossip. Even the advertisements (for everything from GeoVoter map application software to a source for polysleeve yard signs) make good reading.

Campaign Training Institutes

The magazine *Campaigns and Elections* sponsors training seminars for professional consultants and citizen wannabes on topics such as campaign management, media handling and shaping public opinion, election law, etc. They are held in major cities around the country. In 1999 registration was about $300 for a one-day event, plus lodging, meals, and transportation.

University extension services also often run campaign training programs. For example, the University of California Extension has an annual three-day seminar at the U.C. Davis campus that is now in its fifteenth year. Look for advertisements for these institutes in state political magazines and the Extension catalog.

Notes

Chapter 1

1. Fred Register, Fred Register and Associates, Altadena, California. Interview with author, March 15, 1999.

Chapter 2

1. Catherine Lew, Lew-Edwards Group, Oakland, California. Discussion with author, April 1999.

Chapter 3

1. Celinda C. Lake with Pat Callbeck Harper, *Public Opinion Polling: A Handbook for Public Interest and Citizen Advocacy Groups* (Washington, D.C.: Island Press, for the Montana Alliance for Progressive Policy, 1987).

2. The author is very grateful to Colleen Foster, director of the Stockton–San Joaquin County Public Library, and Gene Bregman of Gene Bregman and Associates, Public Opinion and Marketing Research, San Francisco, California, for extensive information on conducting polls, on how polling firms operate, and advice from both a librarian and a pollster on the relationship between the client and the polling consultant.

3. "Wording and Context of Questions," Chapter 3 in Herbert Asher's *Polling and the Public: What Every Citizen Should Know* (see below), is a thorough examination of the problems of question design. There are many other sources on this subject.

4. Based on material in "Report on a Survey of 400 Likely November 1996 Voters Throughout Santa Cruz County," prepared by Gene Bregman and Associates, November 1, 1995.

5. Benton Foundation. *Buildings, Books, and Bytes—Libraries and Communities in the Digital Age.* A report of research conducted by the Benton Foundation with support from the W. K. Kellogg Foundation, published in November 1996.

6. Chapter 9, "Analysis," in *Public Opinion Polling* (see note 1 above), is a particularly useful short account of analytical terms and the common mistakes made in looking at poll results.

7. Benton Foundation. "The Future's in the Balance: Background and Summary of the Research," in *The Future's in the Balance: A Toolkit for Libraries and Communities in the Digital Age.* The toolkit (1998), made possible with support from the W. K. Kellogg Foundation, is part of a program of communications research designed to help libraries more effectively galvanize public support.

8. Herbert Asher, *Polling and the Public: What Every Citizen Should Know,* 4th ed. (Washington, D.C.: Congressional Quarterly, 1998).

9. Jane Farley Templeton, *The Focus Group: A Strategic Guide to Organizing, Conducting, and Analyzing the Focus Group Interview,* rev. ed. (Chicago: Irwin Professional Publishing, 1994).

10. William R. Hamilton, "Political Polling: From the Beginning to the Center of American Election Campaigns," in *Campaigns and Elections American Style,* edited by James A. Thurber and Candice J. Nelson (Westview Press, 1995).

11. Interview with author, January 5, 1999.

Chapter 5

1. Allan Hoffenblum, "Campaign Strategy and Tactics." A lecture prepared for the 1994 Political Campaign Management Institute at University of California, Davis. He is the principal of Allan Hoffenblum & Associates, Political Consulting/Campaign Management in Los Angeles, California.

2. Larry Tramatola Associates, Oakland in 1994 and Santa Cruz in 1996.

Chapter 7

1. *Random House Dictionary,* and *California Journal,* vol. 30, no. 6 (June 1999), p. 6.

2. Catherine A. Golden, *The Campaign Manager—Running and Winning Local Elections* (Ashland, Oregon: Oak Street Press, 1996) pp. 36–37.

3. Murray Fishel, Grassroots Political Campaigns (Northfield, Ohio) at Political Campaign Management Institute, University Extension, University of California, Davis, July 1994.

4. *Ibid.*

5. Golden, *Campaign Manager,* p. 38.

6. Fishel, Grassroots.

7. Interview with Pat Sandidge,

Managing Director, Friends of Santa Cruz Public Libraries, Inc., July 2, 1999.

Chapter 8

1. Derek L. A. Hackett, "Grassroots Fundraising," lecture at Political Campaign Management Institute, University Extension, University of California, Davis, July 1994.

2. *Ibid.*

Chapter 9

1. Derek L. A. Hackett, "Grassroots Fundraising," lecture at Political Campaign Management Institute, University Extension, University of California, Davis, July 1994.

2. Ann Baudry and Robert Schaeffer, *Winning Local and State Elections* (New York: Free Press, 1986), p. 171.

3. Chuck Muth, "How to Use Direct Mail to Raise Money for Any Campaign, Small or Large," *Campaigns and Elections,* May 1998, pp. 51–58.

4. *Ibid.,* p. 55.

Chapter 10

1. Read deButts, "You Make the Call," in *The Road to Victory 2000* 2d ed. (Dubuque, Iowa: Kendall/Hunt, 1998), pp. 360–369.

2. Catherine M. Golden, in her book *The Campaign Manager: Running and Winning Local Elections* (Ashland, Oregon: Oak Street Press, 1996, pp. 39–43), has a different theory about this. She thinks shifts should be one hour each, with an added 15-minute training period, and that the campaign should run two or three shifts per night. See Golden also for examples of reporting forms.

3. Ann Baudry and Bob Schaeffer, *Winning Local and State Elections—The Guide to Organizing Your Campaign* (New York: Free Press, 1986), p. 95.

4. Golden, *Campaign Manager,* pp. 84–87.

Chapter 11

1. The technology of the Internet is developing so rapidly that it is impossible to write much about Web site use that won't be outdated within months. To stay abreast of current trends, read the monthly feature in *Campaigns and Elections* magazine called "Bandwagon: The Complete Guide to Politics on the Web." It includes advice columns from professionals, and Sites of the Month in various categories (Political Consultant, Candidate, Advocacy, etc.).

2. Monroe County Library System, Monroe, Michigan. 1997 Millage Campaign Web Site.

3. "Steve Forbes 2000: He Wants You toWin" (http://www.forbes2000.com/forms/eprinct1.html).

Chapter 12

1. *The Candidate,* Warner Bros., 1972.

2. Judge Lawrence Grey, *How to Win a Local Election* (New York: M. Evans, 1994), p. 172.

3. Howard Kurtz, *Hot Air—All Talk, All the Time* (New York: Times Books, Random House, 1996), p. 131.

4. Grey, *How to Win,* p. 187.

Chapter 13

1. Marilyn Crouch at California State Library Meeting, Santa Barbara, March 3, 1999.

2. Letter of Jack Moore (Lemon Grove), *San Diego Union-Tribune,* February 6, 1999, p. B13.

3. Fred Register, Fred Register and Associates, Altadena, California. Telephone interview with the author, March 15, 1999.

4. Steve Smith, quoted in *The Initiative Cookbook* by Jim Shultz (San Francisco: Democracy Center/Advocacy Institute West, 1996), p. 7.

Chapter 14

1. *The Right Stuff,* Warner Bros., 1983.

2. Joseph Napolitan, "Joseph Napolitan's 100 Greatest Hints," in *The Road to Victory 2000,* p. 27.

Index